CONFESSIONS OF AN OPTIONS STRATEGIST

CONFESSIONS OF AN OPTIONS STRATEGIST
A winner's guide to profitable option trading

ALEXANDER M. GLUSKIN Ph.D.

Hounslow Press

Confessions of An Options Strategist

Copyright © 1985 by Alexander M. Gluskin

All Rights Reserved.

ISBN 0-88882-084-4

Publisher: Anthony Hawke
Editor: Shirley Knight Morris
Designer: Gerard Williams
Composition: Accurate Typesetting Limited
Printer: Gagne Printing Ltd.

Hounslow Press
A Division of
Anthony R. Hawke Limited
124 Parkview Avenue,
Willowdale, Ontario, Canada
M2N 3Y5

Printed in Canada

Second Printing, 1990

Front Cover Photograph by Bill Brooks

Contents

Chapter 1

Introduction

"How would you like to invest $500 and have a good chance of making $2,500?"

The first time I heard this question was in 1976, when stock options were just becoming the newest and the most exciting game in town.

There was no way I could answer "no" to a question like that. I was already deeply interested in the stock market, but the amount of money at my disposal was painfully inadequate for trading stocks on a regular basis. Trying to find an investment vehicle that required smaller initial investment, I had experimented with commodity futures; however, I quickly found out that being locked in on the wrong side of the market was not exactly the best way of having fun!

At that point, options arrived and promised the best of both worlds. They did not require as much money as stocks; they provided good leverage; and they also limited my risk by the amount of my initial investment. What else could one ask for?

I spent a few days reading prospectuses and various introductory literature and a week later I bought my first call option. In less than a month, the option doubled in price. I started getting a vision of myself retiring in a year or two and possibly moving to one of the sunny islands where people do not pay income taxes.

Yet, twelve months later, I was still working as an accountant in Toronto and the move to tropical islands was not even on the horizon. I had bought and sold more than two dozen calls and puts, but I hadn't made a penny for myself. The only person who had benefited from all that activity was my broker. Obviously, I was doing something wrong.

The next step took me to bookstores and libraries. Books on

options were not hard to find, but somehow they did not answer my questions. The first thing I learned was that there were two different kinds of books.

The first type was represented by solid monographs written by the top authorities in the field. Those books listed scores of various strategies, illustrated with tables and diagrams. The only thing I could not find in those books was an indication of how to choose among all those fascinating strategies. I felt like a man with a lot of expensive tools and no instructions for their use.

The books of the second type were much thinner and far more exciting. They illustrated in a step-by-step fashion how the author had made five- or six-digit profits, having started with a minimal investment, in a matter of months. All the trades were supported by photocopies of broker slips and confirmations so as to eliminate any doubts of the author's honesty.

Those books sounded too good to be true. Being an auditor, I went to the old newspapers to double-check the prices and the dates presented in the books. As far as I could ascertain, everything looked authentic.

I followed the advice given in each book as pedantically as humanly possible. My broker made some more money. I lost a few hundred dollars.

I went back to the books and realized that each of the thin get-rich-fast books was preaching one and only one of the strategies listed in the big solid books. I also realized that those isolated strategies worked extremely well during certain periods of time as described in the thin exciting books, but the same strategies proved disastrous during other periods. I also began to suspect that as soon as a strategy stopped working its followers switched from trading to writing books.

This new understanding was very useful in preventing further losses, but it fell short of opening the door to profits. I needed a different book. What I required was a set of rules and guidelines for using various strategies: *when* I should buy calls, *when* I should buy puts, *when* I should buy or write spreads or straddles. Once I had chosen a particular strategy, I had to know *which* of the options to use in order to maximize my profits and to minimize my losses.

Such a book did not exist; therefore, I kept plugging on my own. Slowly but surely my track record was getting better. The day came when my accumulated profits surpassed the total commissions earned by my broker on my trading. I celebrated that day as the first step on the way to victory.

The process of learning accelerated greatly in 1980, when I joined

Burns Fry Limited, a large Canadian brokerage house, as a resident options strategist. By that time my track record was sufficiently good for me to start giving advice and recommendations to the Burns Fry sales force.

Following up on my recommendations, I continued to accumulate information on option strategies. The process of gathering information had speeded up noticeably, because I was giving many more recommendations than I could possibly act on with my own funds.

The pieces of the puzzle were falling into place one by one. The same factors seemed to turn up whenever I had a particularly good winning streak. Other factors turned up together with important mistakes. The trees were gathering into a forest.

Eventually, the picture became so clear that I was able to list all those positive and negative factors on a piece of paper. Once they were all there, it was not too difficult to rephrase them as definite Rules.

As I was re-reading these Rules, I had a dream. How great it would have been had I known all those Rules at the beginning of my trading in 1976! How many hard-earned dollars, sleepless nights and irreversibly destroyed nerve cells I would have saved!

Alas, it is only a dream. We cannot turn the Great Clock of Time backwards. But there was still something I could do with those Rules staring at me from the white sheet of paper. I could share them with other investors and help them save time, money and anguish. By sharing my experience, I could take others through the initial stages much faster and let them use their energy on further exciting discoveries.

This is exactly what this book is all about.

If you have tried investing in options and made spectacular gains in percentage terms that miraculously turned into losses on the bottom line, if you have searched in vain for the key to using all the brilliant strategies, if you have had holes burned in your pockets by the methods which had supposedly made other investors rich, this book is for you.

On the other hand, if you have never touched options before but you are fascinated by them and would like to try them out, this book will still help you. It will aid you in avoiding many costly mistakes and bitter disappointments. It will give you the guidelines to profitable trading and teach you analytical methods that can be applied to any strategy. It will dispel some myths that make investors expect the impossible and take unreasonably high risks.

This book might be somewhat difficult for the beginner. In order to help such readers I have included all the necessary definitions. If you are active in the stock market, you learn very quickly because mistakes cost you money. Some of the Rules in this book might not seem clear to you at the first reading but once you have seen them in action their logic will become transparent. If nothing else, they will prevent you from repeating the same mistakes over and over again.

There are two ways to use this book. The first involves using Chapter 2 as a checklist for trading. Whenever you are going to enter an option transaction, simply go over every single Rule in Chapter 2 and make sure you are not violating any of them. If such is the case, go ahead.

Using the Rules as a checklist will not guarantee, of course, that you become rich overnight or that you incur no losses. Such expectations would be completely unrealistic. What the Rules will do for you is to reduce the probability of large losses and increase your chances for ending up a winner in the long run. In other words, they will load the dice in your favour.

If you decide to follow this route, you might as well ignore the rest of the book. Simply follow the Rules.

The other way to use this book is much closer to my heart. If you are like me, you will never be satisfied with following somebody else's rules. You will want to know where these rules are coming from, why they work and how to create new ones. In that case you should read the entire book. At the end of it you will understand the Rules much better. In addition, you will learn some powerful methods for analyzing various option strategies. Using these methods you will be able to derive new rules from your own experience.

Needless to say, I strongly recommend the second approach, but the choice is yours.

The Rules in Chapter 2 are not the only thing that make this book unique. A quick glance at the list of contents will demonstrate that the classification of strategies is also unusual. Instead of dealing with calls first, puts second, spreads after that, etc., I have classified all the presented strategies by the expected behaviour of the underlying stock. Under this arrangement, we have bullish strategies, bearish strategies, neutral strategies, etc.

This classification reflects the proper order of things. To make money in options, you have to analyze the underlying stock first. Only after that will you be able to select an appropriate option strategy. Without good analysis of stocks, options are practically useless to an investor. This is the central idea of the entire book. It puts the horse before the buggy. In most other books on options, the horse is missing altogether.

Another point of difference is that this book deals primarily with stock options, i.e. the options on the stocks listed on major North American Exchanges. In the last few years options on other financial instruments have been growing faster than mushrooms after a warm rain.

Today an investor has a mind-boggling choice of options on stocks, bonds, commodities, future contracts on commodities, currencies, stock market indices and subindices, and future contracts on stock market indices!

To set the record straight, I have nothing against any of those options. Each one of them can be used to make money if you are familiar enough with the underlying instrument and follow all the principles of investing in options. Only time will tell which of those options will prove useful enough to survive and which will disappear due to the lack of interest.

The reason I devote very little room in this book to all these new options is that there is not much new about them. The analytical methods I apply to stock options are equally valid for all other options. The wording of the Rules might change somewhat, but all the main ideas and methods can be carried over verbatim. In addition, there are numerous books on the market which list and explain the new options in great detail. The authors of those books have done a gigantic job of classifying and summarising all the newly born options. I am grateful to them and very glad that I don't have to duplicate their work.

Yet another feature that sets this book aside is the examples. To begin with, I have used only the examples from real life, because as a lecturer I have found that the favourite stock of option writers, namely XYZ, usually bores the listeners to tears. Real examples, on the contrary, remind the readers about other similar situations they have encountered in their own practice.

Also, since my experience as an investor and strategist covers both the U.S. and Canadian markets, I have included examples from both sides of the border. I hope that will make the book more interesting for the readers in both countries without limiting its usefulness. The rules of the game are practically identical in the U.S. and in Canada, so that the ideas, methods and Rules presented in the book can be applied equally to options trading on any North American Exchange.

The last but not least important characteristic of this book is contained in Chapter 10. That Chapter illustrates the importance of cash management, which has been traditionally overlooked in the option literature. Would you believe that there are many investors who use appropriate strategies, who are right over 60% of the time, and who end up losing all their money due to errors in cash management? It is hard to believe yet it is true. In fact, you can be right in your forecasts of the underlying stocks 99 times out of 100, you can be picking the best possible options to buy or sell, and with all that you can still have a 100% chance to lose all your money if you follow the wrong cash management policy!

Chapter 10 sets the Rules for cash management which will prevent you from being a winner on paper and a loser in real life.

I want to finish this introductory chapter by wishing you, my reader, as much excitement, fun and profits as your nervous system can handle. Options can be anything from a super-conservative investment to an outright gamble. I hope this book will help you to enjoy the game of options to the fullest and will also prevent you from making some grave mistakes along the way.

Good luck!

Chapter 2

Rules

The following Rules do not guarantee profits on any given trade or series of trades. However, following these Rules will make large losses less probable and will tip the scales in your favour in the long run.

1. Never put more money into buying options than you are prepared to lose.

2. You should buy only those options that will expire after the time period during which you expect the underlying stock to reach your target.

3. When buying options, you should select the strike price that produces the highest gain per share in percentage terms when the underlying stock reaches your target.

4. You should buy only those options which will double their purchase price (after commissions) when the underlying stock reaches your target.

5. Selling the options you own is always better than exercising them and then closing the resulting position in the underlying stock.

6. Sell the options you own as soon as the underlying stock has reached your target.

7. Do not sell the options you own at a loss earlier than on the expiration day, unless your forecast of the underlying stock has changed.

8. If you bought options and then your forecast of the underlying stock changed for the worse, sell the options only when you can get 50% or more of the purchase price back (after commis-

sions). If you cannot do that, sell the options on the expiration day.

9. Write only out-of-the-money options which are the closest to being at-the-money.

10. Write only those options that have between 2 and 5 months until expiration.

11. Write only those options whose price is at least 10% of the strike price.

12. When writing puts, place a mental stop-loss at the price which is equal to the price of the underlying stock at the time of writing minus the price of the put.

13. Cover your short positions as soon as you can make a profit (after commissions) equal to 75% of the initial price of the options.

14. If your forecast of the underlying stock has changed unfavourably, close all short positions immediately.

15. If you wrote options with the intention of buying them back later, and they were exercised, immediately close the resulting stock position.

16. When writing uncovered options, the amount of money you receive should not exceed the amount of money you are prepared to lose.

17. A put owner should never move down his original target for the underlying stock. The profit should be taken as soon as the original target is reached.

18. Before writing uncovered calls, make sure that the underlying stock is not a potential take-over candidate.

19. When writing calls, place a mental stop-loss at the price which is equal to the price of the underlying stock at the time of writing plus the price of the call.

20. You should buy straddles only when the price of the underlying stock is within one dollar of the strike price.

21. You should buy only those straddles that will make a 50% profit (after commissions) when the underlying stock reaches one of your targets.

22. If you own a straddle or a combination, and the underlying stock has reached one of your targets, you must sell the option which is making a profit and keep the other option.

23. When writing a straddle, place one mental stop-loss at the

price equal to the strike price plus the total amount received for the straddle, and another mental stop-loss at the price equal to the strike price minus the total amount received for the straddle.

24. Write only those straddles whose total price is at least 15% of the strike price.

25. Write straddles only when the price of the underlying stock is within one dollar of the strike price.

26. Cover your short straddles and combinations as soon as you can make a profit (after commissions) equal to 50% of the total amount received for the straddle or combination.

27. If one side of your short straddle or combination has been exercised, immediately buy back the other side and close the resulting stock position.

28. When writing a combination, place one mental stop-loss at the price equal to the higher strike price plus the total amount received for the combination, and another mental stop-loss at the price equal to the lower strike price minus the total amount received for the combination.

29. Write only those combinations whose total price is at least 10% of the lower strike price.

30. In most cases, writing calls against the stock and buying them back will yield smaller profits than buying and selling the stock itself on the same days.

31. If you would like to trade short-term swings in the stock you own, but you cannot afford to sell the stock because of taxes, you should trade call options against that stock.

32. Never write calls against a stock which is outright bearish.

33. You should buy puts against a long position in the underlying stock only if you could sell the stock and buy corresponding calls without violating any of the Rules applicable to calls. (Tax considerations might provide exceptions to this Rule.)

34. If you would like to hold a risky stock several weeks longer for tax purposes, consider buying puts against it.

35. If you expect a quick recovery in the stock which you otherwise would have sold for tax purposes, sell the stock and buy calls.

36. If you would like to buy a stock but the funds will become available only several months later, consider buying calls in order to fix the price of the stock.

37. If you intend to purchase a stock by exercising calls and if the interest on the cash is greater than the dividends on the stock, do it on the expiration day.

38. Writing puts is always preferable to simultaneous covered writing.

39. Writing calls against a stock is not a good way to sell the stock.

40. Writing uncovered puts is not a good way to buy the underlying stock.

41. Do not use spreads.

42. Your initial investment in options, measured by the amount you are prepared to lose, should not exceed 15% of the total capital available for options.

43. You should invest the same number of dollars (measured by the amount you are prepared to lose) into buying or writing uncovered options until you have doubled your total capital available for options.

44. When you have doubled the total capital available for options for the first time, you should remove half of it and withdraw it from investing in options.

45. When you have doubled the total capital available for options for the second, third, etc., time, you should double the amount you are prepared to lose.

Chapter 3

Basic Definitions

This chapter contains definitions of the terms used throughout the book. Since this book was not planned as an exhaustive handbook of options, I did not try to include *all* the definitions that one might find in option literature. If you are a beginner as far as options are concerned, your broker will send you an option Prospectus which you must read and understand before you can start buying and selling options. Not only does it make sense to read the Prospectus before you enter your first trade, but it is also required by law that you do so. The Prospectus will explain all that a beginner has to know, will provide examples of various strategies and will stress the risks related to trading options. I strongly recommend that you read the Prospectus before reading this book and that you refer back to the Prospectus if something in this book seems unclear.

I have taken the liberty of defining some of the option terms differently from the standard definitions. In every case, the meaning of the term is exactly the same under my definition and under the generally accepted one. My choice of definitions was based on the descriptive qualities of various definitions. While most of the authors use verbal descriptions of mathematical formulae to define such terms as *in-the-money*, *out-of-the-money*, etc., I prefer the definitions which relate the option to the underlying stock. It does not change the meaning of the term, but it defines it more descriptively.

Let us start with the definition of a *call option*, or simply a *call*. A call option is the right to buy a stock at a fixed price during a fixed interval of time. For example, an IBM May 120 call is a contract that entitles its owner to buy 100 shares of IBM at $120 US per share at any time before the closing of the market on the third Friday in May.

In this particular example IBM is called *the underlying stock*, the fixed price of $120 US is called *the exercise price* or *the strike price,* the month of May is called *the expiration month,* and the third Friday in May is called *the expiration date.*

In fact, the official time when options expire is later than the closing of the market on the third Friday of the expiration month, as you will find out if you ever write the exam to become licenced as an option broker. Moreover, the official expiration time might be differ-ent in Canada and the United States. But for all practical purposes you can consider the closing of the market on the third Friday of the expiration month to be the expiry date. Since this book deals exclusively with practical aspects of trading options, we can use the above definition and not bother with legal nuances.

The name itself, "a call option", comes from the fact that the owner of such a contract has the right "to call the stock away" from the issuer of the contract. Indeed, if you have the right to buy 100 shares of IBM at $120 US, then somebody out there must be under the obligation to sell those shares to you upon request. The person who undertakes such an obligation is called *the writer of the call option.*

To illustrate the position of the writer of a call option, let us consider the following chain of events. Mr. Jones buys 100 shares of Alcan at $25 Cdn. and holds the stock for several months. When Alcan reaches $43 Cdn., Mr. Jones is almost ready to sell the stock. Almost, but not quite yet. He believes that Alcan will soon be trading above $45 Cdn., at which time he would be more than happy to sell his shares. Mr. Jones turns his attention to call options and finds out that there are willing buyers of Alcan February 45 calls at $3 Cdn. per share. Now Mr. Jones quickly makes up his mind. He *writes* (or, in other words, *issues*) a February 45 call on Alcan. This call is purchased by a Mr. Smith, who pays $3. Cdn. per share for it. Consequently, Mr. Jones receives the $3 Cdn. per share.

After this transaction, Mr. Smith owns the Alcan February 45 call, and he is said to be *long the call.* He has the right to exercise this call. If he decides to exercise, he will buy 100 shares of Alcan from Mr. Jones at the fixed price of $45 Cdn. When Mr. Smith purchased his call, he paid *the price* (or *the premium*) of $3 Cdn. per share.

Mr. Jones, who sold this call to Mr. Smith, is said to be *short the call.* Since he gave Mr. Smith the right to buy Alcan from him at $45 Cdn., he is now under the obligation to sell the stock for $45 Cdn. on demand. Even if the market price of Alcan runs up to $100 Cdn., Mr. Smith will be able to force Mr. Jones to sell the stock at $45 Cdn. However, Mr. Jones is sure that he will be happy to sell his 100 shares of Alcan at any price above $45 Cdn. Meanwhile he has received $3 Cdn. per share from Mr. Smith.

Several weeks later Alcan was trading at $49 Cdn. Mr. Smith took a hard look at his February 45 call and decided that he didn't want to hold it any longer; however, he was not eager to exercise the call because he did not really want to own 100 shares of Alcan. He doubted if the stock had much upside potential.

Through his broker Mr. Smith found out that not everybody agreed with him. In fact, there were willing buyers for Alcan February 45 calls at the price of $5 Cdn. per share. Mr. Smith sold his call to a Mr. Adams, who obviously believed that Alcan was going at least a few dollars higher.

We will analyze the strategies employed by Mr. Jones, Mr. Smith and Mr. Adams in other chapters of this book. This chapter deals with definitions rather than strategies, and I have brought up this example to illustrate the difference between *writing options* and *selling options*.

Let us examine the two transactions more closely. At first they look very similar: in the first transaction, Mr. Jones sold one February 45 call on Alcan to Mr. Smith. In the second, Mr. Smith sold one Alcan February 45 call to Mr. Adams; however, this similarity is misleading.

Before the first transaction neither Mr. Jones nor Mr. Smith owned an Alcan February 45 call. After the transaction Mr. Smith owned the call and, therefore, had the right to buy the stock from Mr. Jones. Mr. Jones was short the same call and was under the obligation to sell the stock to Mr. Smith on demand. In effect, the transaction between these two gentlemen resulted in a birth of one Alcan February 45 call. Under such circumstances Mr. Jones is called *a writer*, as opposed to *a seller*, of the call.

In the second transaction, Mr. Smith sold to Mr. Adams the call he had owned previously. After the sale Mr. Smith had no more right to purchase 100 shares of Alcan at $45 Cdn. from anyone, nor was he under any obligation with respect to Alcan shares. If Mr. Adams decided to exercise his call now, he would be buying 100 Alcan shares at $45 Cdn. from Mr. Jones, the original writer. Since the sale of the Alcan February 45 call to Mr. Adams left Mr. Smith under no obligation whatsoever, he would be called *a seller*, as opposed to *a writer*.

In short, the original issuer of an option is called *a writer*, while a person who first buys an option and then re-sells it is called *a seller*. Unfortunately, the two terms are often used in the literature as if they were synonymous.

The examples presented above involved option transactions between individuals. If Mr. Smith decided to exercise his Alcan

February 45 call instead of selling it, he would have to find Mr. Jones and demand the Alcan shares from him. This used to be the case many years ago, when options were traded only over-the-counter. At present, all the option trades are made between the investor and an option clearing corporation. In our example, Mr. Jones would have written one Alcan February 45 call to a clearing corporation, while Mr. Smith would have bought the same call from the clearing corporation. The only difference between doing the transaction directly through a clearing corporation is that in the later case Mr. Smith or his broker would not have to locate Mr. Jones in order to exercise the call. Nor would they have to sue Mr. Jones if he refused to honour the option contract and to sell 100 shares of Alcan for $45 Cdn. Having bought the call from the clearing corporation, Mr. Smith would be dealing with the corporation and let it worry about possible problems related to the original writer.

It is important to realize, however, that a clearing corporation acts only as a middle man. It does not buy, write, or sell options for its own account. Before entering into a transaction, it finds the two sides and then acts as an intermediary.

Let us now return to Mr. Jones for a moment. When he wrote the Alcan February 45 call and, therefore, undertook the obligation to sell 100 shares of Alcan at $45 Cdn. on demand, he actually owned the stock. Many investors who have not had much experience with options believe that one must own the stock before he can write call options against it. In fact, it is not true. As a car dealer can undertake the obligation to deliver a car to the buyer while he does not yet have the car in the stockroom, so an investor can write a call option without owning the underlying stock.

In our example, Mr. Jones could write the Alcan February 45 call without owning 100 shares of Alcan. If the call was exercised at a later day, Mr. Jones would have to deliver the stock and sell it for $45 Cdn. He would have a choice between two different courses of action. First, he could buy Alcan at whatever price existed in the market and deliver the shares to the call owner. Second, he could deliver the shares establishing a short position in Alcan for himself. (If you are not familiar with selling stocks short, I urge you to learn about it before continuing with this book. You cannot understand options if you are not comfortable with shorting.) We will study the strategy of writing calls while not owning the underlying stock in Chapter 6.

So far, we have been discussing call options only. These are options to buy. The only other kind of options is *put options* (or simply *puts*). Puts are options to sell. For example, a February 40 put on Imperial Oil gives its owner the right to sell 100 shares of Imperial Oil at the fixed price of $40 Cdn. per share at any time before the closing of the market on the third Friday in February. The buyer of the put would have to pay *a price* (or, in other words, *a premium*) for it. Once he purchased the put, he would be said to be *long the put*.

The initial issuer, or *the writer*, of the same put would undertake the obligation to buy 100 shares of Imperial Oil at the price of $40 Cdn. at any time before the closing of the market on the third Friday in February. The writer would receive *a price* (or *a premium*) from the buyer. He would be said to be *short the put*. A person who first bought a put and later sold it would not be *a writer*, but rather *a seller* of the put. As a result of the selling transaction he would own no right and would be under no obligation with respect to the Imperial Oil shares.

As in the case of call options, it does not matter if the buyer, the writer, or the seller of a put option actually own the shares of the underlying stock.

Why is a put called "a put"? — because the owner of the put has the right "to put the stock to the writer", i.e. to force the writer to buy the stock from him.

Now we can summarize the legal position of buyers and writers of calls and puts in a table as follows:

	call	put
buyer	right to buy	right to sell
writer	obligation to sell	obligation to buy

As the above table shows, the buyers acquire certain rights, while the writers undertake certain obligations. It is only fair that the buyers pay for their rights while the writers collect money from the buyers for the uncertainty and the inconvenience of being under an obligation. This is but a minor manifestation of the general Law of Nature which reads:

THERE IS NO FREE LUNCH.

Let us take a closer look at the prices paid for options. Remember the transaction between Mr. Smith and Mr. Adams, when the first gentleman sold one Alcan February 45 call to the second gentleman for $5 Cdn. per share? At that time Alcan was trading at $49 Cdn. What did Mr. Adams pay $5 Cdn. for?

Before we answer that question, we should examine the courses of action open to an option holder. At any time he can do one of the three things: sell the option, exercise it, or do nothing. Since one does not make a profit by doing nothing, sooner or later the option holder would have to sell or exercise his option.

It is obvious that Mr. Adams was not going to sell the option immediately to someone else for the same $5 Cdn. per share. Even ignoring broker's commissions and floor spreads, he would not have made any money by buying and selling the option at the same price. Let us see if he could fare better by exercising the call. Exercising would mean buying 100 shares of Alcan at $45 Cdn. per share. Mr. Adams could immediately sell the shares for $49 Cdn. in the market and end up with a profit of $49 − $45 = $4 Cdn. per share on the stock alone (we are ignoring commissions). Since he had paid $5 Cdn. for the call and made only $4 Cdn. on the stock, he would end up with a loss of $1 Cdn. per share.

The $4 Cdn. that Mr. Adams could make on the stock by exercising the call and selling the stock, is called *the intrinsic value of the call.* So why did he pay as much as $5 Cdn. for a call whose intrinsic value was only $4 Cdn.? Obviously, he must have believed that future developments would result in increases in either the intrinsic value of his call, or its market price, or both. Because of these expectations of favourable developments in the future, the difference between the total price of $5 Cdn. and the intrinsic value of $4 Cdn. is called *the time value of the call.* The time value of the Alcan February 45 call, which was selling at $5 Cdn., when Alcan was trading at $49 Cdn., was equal to $1 Cdn.

The time value of the same call at a different time, namely when it was purchased by Mr. Smith from Mr. Jones, was zero. Indeed, when Mr. Smith bought the call, Alcan was trading at $43 Cdn. By exercising the call Mr. Smith would have bought 100 shares of Alcan at $45 Cdn. and the best price he could get for the shares in the market was $43 Cdn. Going ahead with that transaction would have resulted in a loss of $2 Cdn. per share. In other words, no profit could be made on the stock by exercising the February 45 call, when Alcan was trading at $43 Cdn. Therefore, its intrinsic value was zero. It follows that the entire price of $3 Cdn. which Mr. Smith paid for the call represented the time value.

When the intrinsic value of an option is positive, such an option is said to be *in-the-money.* For example, the Alcan February 45 call was *in-the-money by $4 Cdn.,* when Alcan was trading at $49 Cdn. When intrinsic value is zero, the option is said to be *out-of-the-money,* unless the stock price is exactly the same as the strike price, in which case the option is said to be *at-the-money.* When Alcan was trading at $43 Cdn., the February 45 call was *out-of-the-money,* but when Alcan reached $45 Cdn., the call became *at-the-money.*

All these definitions apply to puts as well as to calls. For example, a February 40 put on Imperial Oil would have *the intrinsic value* of $2 Cdn. when the underlying stock traded at $38 Cdn. Why? — Because the owner of this put could exercise it, therefore selling 100 shares of Imperial Oil for $40 Cdn. As a result he would find himself short 100 shares and he could cover the short position by buying the same number of shares in the market at $38 Cdn. His profit on the stock transaction would be $40 − $38 = $2 Cdn. per share (before commissions). That profit would represent the intrinsic value of the put. If at the same time the February 40 put was trading at $3 Cdn., then the difference between the price of the put (i.e. $3 Cdn.) and its intrinsic value (i.e. $2 Cdn.) would represent *the time value* of the put (in this case $1 Cdn.).

If Imperial Oil traded at $41 Cdn. instead of $38 Cdn., the intrinsic value of the February 40 put would be zero and the entire price of the put would represent its time value. To check it, all you have to do is to imagine that the owner of the put exercised it and then covered the resulting short position in the stock by buying the shares in the market. After the exercise, the former owner of the put would be short the stock at $40 Cdn. Buying the shares in the market at $41 Cdn. would result in a loss of $41 − $40 = $1 Cdn.

Consequently, we would say that the February 40 put was *in-the-money* by $2 Cdn., when Imperial Oil traded at $38 Cdn., was *out-of-the-money* when Imperial Oil was trading at $41 Cdn., and was *at-the-money* when Imperial Oil traded at $40 Cdn. even.

If some of the concepts presented in this chapter are new to you, I suggest that you study them on a number of examples of your own. These concepts represent the language of options and will be extensively used throughout the book. From now on reading this book will be somewhat similar to travelling in a foreign country. It makes sense to master the language before you venture out into the streets and try to communicate with strangers!

Chapter 4

Confessions

Having read this far, you might be wondering why I called this book *Confessions of an Options Strategist*. In this chapter I will try to answer your question. I will share with you my most important discoveries about options and I will show how far the truth is from the popular myths. Together with myths, many unreasonable expectations will turn to dust and disappear in the wind. Under the dust you will discover a totally new approach to making money in options, the one that really works.

The first myth we have to dispel happens to be the most damaging of all. Scores of investors turn to options when they realize that they cannot make consistent profits buying and selling stocks. They switch to options because they believe that the magic of options can somehow replace the hard work of forecasting the movements of stocks. When they meet me and find out that I am an option strategist, they always say: "Lucky you! You don't care what stocks are doing, right? You keep making money in options come hell or high water!"

Nothing could be further from the truth.

Let us look at a few examples. If you bought a Bell Canada May 20 call on August 31, 1982 and paid $0.50 Cdn. per share for it, in nine months you could sell the call at a fantastic profit. To be more specific, on May 9, 1983, you could sell your call for $8.00 Cdn. Your profit on the call (before commissions) would have been 1,500% !

The reason for such a dramatic gain was that the price of Bell Canada had increased from $18.50 Cdn. on August 31, 1982 to $28.00 Cdn. on May 9, 1983. The 51% increase in the price of the underlying stock translated into the staggering 1,500% increase in the price of the call option.

Another example. If you bought a Mitel June 40 call on January 5, 1983 at $3.75 Cdn., you would have suffered watching it decline in value to $0.10 Cdn. four months later. You would never have recovered any significant portion of your investment, since the price of the call remained at or below $0.10 Cdn. until expiration.

The reason was quite simple. Mitel started to decline right after you bought the call and proceeded to fall to $5.25 Cdn.! As the stock tumbled, its June 40 calls rapidly became useless.

I could bring up more examples that would include calls, puts, spreads, straddles and other fancy strategies, but I don't see much need for that. I hope that my point is clear already:

IT IS THE MOVEMENT OF THE UNDERLYING STOCK
THAT CREATES PROFITS OR LOSSES ON OPTIONS.

No matter how much you know about options, if you ignore the underlying stocks in designing your strategy, you will be severely punished. It happens every day to numerous investors who hope that mathematical complexities of option strategies will allow them to avoid studying the underlying stocks and will generate profits irrespective of what the stocks are doing. Alas, there is only one such strategy and it can be used only by professional traders who do not pay commissions. This strategy is called "conversions" and its use by professional traders has important implications for option prices and for relationships between various other option strategies. Conversions are covered in chapter 11. Until you come to that chapter, all you have to know about them is that as an investor you cannot use them; therefore, you absolutely have to know something about the stock before you can make money on its options. It is my first and most important Confession:

Confession 1: IN ORDER TO MAKE MONEY IN OPTIONS,
YOU MUST HAVE A REASONABLE FORECAST
OF THE BEHAVIOUR OF THE UNDERLYING STOCK.

I want you to pay attention to the word "behaviour" in this Confession. I had a good reason for choosing this word instead of "price" or "direction". The fact is that you can make money in options even if you don't know whether the underlying stock is going to move higher or lower. There are strategies that will help you to make a profit if you can forecast a change in volatility of the stock without specifying the direction of the next move. These strategies are analyzed in Chapter 7.

Expecting a change in the volatility of the stock, however, is a way of forecasting its behaviour, isn't it? Of course, saying that the stock will become much more volatile is quite different from saying that it will move to higher levels, but nevertheless it is also a forecast. And such a forecast can only be made based on some information about the stock.

If you know nothing about the stock, that is exactly what you should expect to make on any option strategy related to that stock — nothing!

Okay, so you have to forecast stocks, options or no options. It comes as a great disappointment for anyone who hoped to avoid stock forecasting by using options, but most of the investors discover this fact sooner or later and learn to live with it.

What is the next step?

Let us say you have found a stock that you expect to move up. Is this sufficient information for going ahead and buying calls on the stock? Most investors do exactly that. And quite often end up losing money.

Here is an example of how it happens. On June 24, 1983, Tenneco was trading at $41.50 US and the stock looked rather promising. February 45 calls on Tenneco were trading at $2.00 US, reflecting the optimism of investors.

On January 27, 1984, Tenneco was trading at $42.00 US, which was $0.50 US higher than on June 24. The gain was small, but nevertheless it was a gain. On the same day February 45 calls were trading at $0.13 US. While the stock had moved slightly higher, the calls had managed to lose practically all their initial value!

This is what happens to so many option buyers. They often happen to be right on the stock, but still end up with losses on their options. I have had my share of such losses, which lead me to what I call my Second Confession:

Confession 2: BEING RIGHT ON THE STOCK
IS NOT ENOUGH TO MAKE A PROFIT ON ITS OPTIONS.

Forecasting the behaviour of the stock is only the first step on the way to profitable investing in options. Step two is selecting an option strategy best suited for the expected behaviour of the stock.

One of the attractive features of options is the great variety of possible strategies. By buying some options and selling others at the same time, you can create an unlimited number of combinations and permutations. Mathematicians and computer specialists are drawn by that complexity as irresistibly as moths to the light of a candle.

Unfortunately, the analogy holds true to the end. The most complex strategies are the least probable to bring any profits whatsoever.

The reason for that is simple. The more options you are buying and selling at the same time, the more you limit your potential profits and the more commissions you are paying in the process.

In Chapter 9 you will find my analysis of spreads, which has led me to a blank recommendation not to use them under any circumstances. The arguments presented in Chapter 9 apply to all other "fancy" strategies.

In more general terms, here is my Third Confession:

Confession 3: SIMPLE STRATEGIES WORK BEST.

Now I would like to return to the very beginning of this book, to the question about investing $500 in order to make $2,500. If a mathematically inclined mind is attracted by the complexity of options, it becomes completely hypnotized by the use of leverage!

When you happen to buy the right option on the right stock at the right time, you more than double your money. As soon as it happened to me more than once, I quickly figured out that starting with $1,000 and doubling it every 3 months I would become a millionaire in two and a half years!

The combination of leverage with compounding was a magic brush that painted my eyeglasses in bright pink. I was flying high, having completely forgotten that the higher you fly, the harder you fall.

Fortunately, I did not fall from cloud nine. I was barely climbing cloud three, when two big losses in a row brought me down abruptly and buried my face in thick mud.

I stopped investing for a while and took a very close look at the use of leverage. The discovery I made had an effect that reminded me of the cold showers I used to take every morning many years ago. I checked and re-checked my logic and my calculations, but I could not find a flaw. There wasn't one. That discovery became my Fourth Confession:

Confession 4: THE MORE LEVERAGE YOU USE, THE HIGHER
YOUR CHANCES
OF LOSING YOUR ENTIRE CAPITAL.

To illustrate why this is true, imagine that you have such a good method of picking stocks and call options that you are right 99 times out of 100. Imagine also that you double your money when you are right and lose the entire amount invested if you are wrong. Even under these unrealistically favourable conditions, if you keep reinvesting all your profits, you will eventually lose all your money to the last penny!

Indeed, no matter how many times you have been right, all your money remains invested in the next trade. Sooner or later you will be wrong. Once you have missed, your entire capital will be gone and you will not be able to continue. Some investors believe that such a disaster can be avoided if one were smart enough to withdraw a certain portion of the profits after the first few profitable trades. The flaw in this argument lies in the fact that even with the batting average of 99%, you are not guaranteed that your first or second trade will be profitable. If you start by investing all or most of your money and you miss on the first trade, you are finished. All you are doing by using a lot of leverage is inviting a lot of trouble.

So how much leverage should one use? The answer to this question can be found in Chapter 10, which is devoted to cash management. As a matter of fact, I believe that sound cash management is *more* important than the choice of strategy. Even if your strategy or forecasting ability is average, the use of proper cash management techniques will preserve a significant portion of your capital. At the same time, even the best strategy coupled with poor cash management will lead to a disaster, as illustrated above.

The proper use of leverage is one of the facets of sound cash management.

I have to make my last confession: this chapter has turned out to be rather depressing. Four beautiful myths about options have been shattered one after another. The entire attraction of options seems to be gone. At this point you might be tempted to close this book, throw it away, and never look at options again.

Before you do it, go back to Chapter 2 and take another glance at the Rules. They are your guidelines to profits. They will show you how to avoid the hidden dangers and will help you to capture elusive opportunities. This book is about making money in options, not losing it.

It is necessary, however, to destroy the old myths before one can build a sound foundation for a different approach. You must have heard that most investors who trade options lose money. It is true. The reason for their losses is their belief in the old myths. The very fact that they lose money is proof that their beliefs are wrong.

My Confessions opened my eyes to what was really happening with options, why the generally accepted views were incorrect, and how one could tip the scales in one's favour.

The following chapters will present analyses of the most important strategies and the best ways of using them. Now that the myths have been dispelled, the road to profits is clear!

Chapter 5

Recommended Strategies — Bullish
1. Buying Calls
2. Writing Puts

When you are bullish on a stock and you want to use options on that stock, there are two simple strategies you can use. First, you can buy calls on the stock. Second, you can write puts. In either case, I assume that you do not own the underlying stock, nor are you interested in owning it. All you want to do is make a profit on options when the stock goes up.

These two simple strategies are my favourites. As stated in my Third Confession, simple strategies work best.

There are other popular bullish strategies, including bullish spreads and simultaneous covered writing. In my experience, they are inferior to buying calls or writing puts. These inferior strategies are analyzed in Chapter 9. By the way, if you have heard or read that simultaneous covered writing is a "neutral" strategy, I will prove to you in Chapter 9 that it is not so.

For the time being, let us leave polemics to Chapter 9 and start with the analyses of the two recommended bullish strategies.

1. Buying Calls

You might have heard that most call buyers lose money and, therefore, that call buyers as a group end up losers. This popular opinion is nothing more than another myth.

Curiously enough, the first statement is correct: the majority of call buyers lose money. The popular conclusion, however, is incorrect: the call buyers as a group are not losers! Sounds like a contradiction?

To illustrate what is really happening to buyers of calls, consider the following example: on October 22, 1982, four friends decided to enter the option market. Since they were all bullish on the economy, the stock market, and the world in general, they all bought call options. Each of them, however, bought calls on his favourite stock. Following their usual competitive spirit, each of the four friends invested equal amounts of money (as close as they could) in his calls in order to see who would end up the biggest winner.

Mr. White bought 28 Baker International June 30 calls at $1.75 US and paid $5,110.00 US, including commissions.

Mr. Green bought 6 Eastman Kodak July 95 calls at $8.00 US and paid $4,915.00 US, including commissions.

Mr. Brown bought 40 Global Marine June 15 calls at $1.25 US and paid $5,260.00 US, including commissions.

Mr. Black bought 16 Marriott Corp. July 55 calls at $3.00 US and paid $4,965.00 US, including commissions.

The friends decided that the biggest winner would give a big party to celebrate their investment wisdom and financial success.

On May 13, 1983, Mr. Black sold his calls for $19.00 US and pocketed $30,200.00 US. His net profit amounted to $30,200.00 − $4,965.00 = $25,235.00 US.

On June 17, 1983, Mr. White's calls expired worthless. Even though Mr. White lost his entire investment of $5,110.00 US, he took the loss philosophically.

On the same day Mr. Brown's calls also expired worthless, taking with them his entire investment of $5,260.00 US. Mr. Brown responded to the lose by changing his broker.

On July 15, 1983, Mr. Green's calls expired worthless. His total loss amounted to $4,915.00 US. Mr. Green swore never to play the stock market again and later that day was stopped by police and charged with impaired driving.

Remembering the old agreement, Mr. Black gave a big party, but his old friends Messrs. White, Green and Brown failed to show up.

Emotions notwithstanding, the four gentlemen did not do so badly. Despite the fact that three of them ended up big losers while only one made a profit, as a group they were certainly ahead. Their total investment of

$$\$5,110.00 + \$4,915.00 + \$5,260.00 + \$4,965.00 = \$20,250.00 \text{ US}$$

turned into $30,200.00 US, all of which found its way into Mr. Black's bank account. As a group, the former friends made a profit of $9,950.00 US!

As you can see, the fact that the majority of call buyers lose money does not automatically mean that they also lose as a group. If the gains of the winners are larger than the losses of the losers, the entire group might break even or make a profit. The most important point is that the game of buying calls is not stacked against the buyer.

Another popular belief is that since most options are not exercised (which is true), the buyers of those options must lose money (which is not true at all). The following example will show the flaw in the logic of the above statement.

On June 19, 1984, Ms. Short wrote 5 Imperial Oil February 35 calls, which were bought by Ms. Tall at $4.25 Cdn. Two months later, on August 21, 1984, Ms. Tall sold her calls for $5.50 Cdn. The buyer of the calls just happened to be Ms. Short, the original writer of these calls.

After the second transaction, Ms. Tall did not own any calls. Instead, she had a profit of $1.25 Cdn. (ignoring commissions). The books of Ms. Short were also balanced. She had been short the calls from the day she wrote them until the day she bought them back. Her loss equalled Ms. Tall's gain (ignoring commissions).

These 5 Imperial Oil February 35 calls were born on June 19, 1984, and disappeared on August 21, 1984. They would never be exercised and, therefore, would eventually show up in the statistics of unexercised calls. But does it mean that the buyer, Ms. Tall, lost any money? Not at all!

The point here is that most options are neither exercised nor expire worthless. They disappear in closing transactions, when the books of buyers and writers balance out. Profits and losses of option buyers are in no way related to the percentage of options exercised.

As you can see, buying calls in not such a losing proposition as some writers and speakers would make you believe. It is definitely not a game where the odds against you are so high that no amount of skill would keep your head above the water. Far from it. In fact, following all the Rules in Chapter 2 will make buying calls a very profitable strategy.

To get better acquainted with this strategy, imagine that you bought a Brunswick Corp. December 35 call on August 22, 1984. Your cost would be $3.25 US per share (ignoring commissions). How much money could you make on this call and how much could you lose?

First, I would like to remind you of an important fact discovered in Chaper 4:

IT IS THE MOVEMENT OF THE UNDERLYING STOCK
THAT CREATES PROFITS OR LOSSES ON OPTIONS.

Therefore, to analyze potential profits and losses on your

Brunswick Corp. December 35 call, we have to consider possible movements of the underlying stock, i.e. Brunswick Corp.

When you bought your call on August 22, 1984, the stock was trading at $32.25 US. What would happen if it moved to $40.00 US? In order to realize a profit, you would either have to sell your call or exercise it. If you decided to sell it, you would have to accept the price existing in the market at that time. What that price would be, nobody can tell in advance. It would depend on the speed with which Brunswick Corp. moved up from $35.25 US to $40.00 US, on the amount of time left until expiration, and on the general level of enthusiasm among option buyers at that time.

Unlike the selling price, the profit on exercising the call can be calculated in advance with a hundred per cent precision. Indeed, by exercising the call, you would buy 100 shares of Brunswick Corp. at $35.00 US. You could then sell those shares immediately for $40.00 US in the market. Your gain on the sale of the stock would be $40.00 − $35.00 = $5.00 US per share, which is equal to *the intrinsic value* of your call at that time as defined in Chapter 3.

One good thing about the intrinsic value is that it can be easily calculated in advance if one knows the strike price and the price of the underlying stock. Another good thing is that the intrinsic value can be used as a conservative estimate of the market price of the option. The reason for that is that option prices practically never fall more than $0.50 below the intrinsic value. To illustrate why, let us imagine for a moment that a Brunswick Corp. December 35 call could be bought at $4.00 US when Brunswick Corp. was trading at $40.00 US. The buyer of that call could immediately exercise the call, sell the stock and make a $5.00 US profit as described above. Since he would have paid only $4.00 US for the call, he would end up with a net profit of $1.00 US before commissions.

This is exactly what happens. As soon as the price of the call declines as much as $0.25 − $0.50 below its intrinsic value, professional option traders, who do not pay commissions, start buying these calls, exercising them and making small profits without any risk. Their buying prevents the call prices from declining further.

In analyzing any option strategy, I always use intrinsic values as a conservative estimate of the option price in the future. Returning to our example, we will assume that when Brunswick Corp. was trading at $40.00 US, the price of its December 35 calls would be at least $5.00 US. Therefore, you could sell your call for at least $5.00 US per share and, since your cost had been $3.25 US, you would have made a profit of $5.00 − $3.25 = $1.75 US per share (all that assuming that we ignore commissions, which we do).

What if instead of rallying to $40.00 US, Brunswick Corp. declined to $30.00 US? In that case the intrinsic value of your call would become zero since it would make no sense at all to exercise the call. Indeed, why would you want to buy Brunswick Corp. at $35.00 US through exercise, when you could buy it in the market at $30.00 US? The intrinsic value of zero is our best conservative estimate of the price of the call. True, you might have been able to sell it to some wild optimist for a few pennies, but we cannot rely on that in our analysis. Therefore, we assume that you couldn't sell the call and wouldn't exercise it either. This means that you would have lost your entire investment of $3.25 US per share.

Repeating similar calculations of your profits and losses at various prices of Brunswick Corp., we could fill in the table as in Figure 1.

Another way to present the same information is to draw a graph in which the horizontal axis represents the prices of Brunswick Corp., while the vertical axis represents a profit or a loss as in Figure 2:

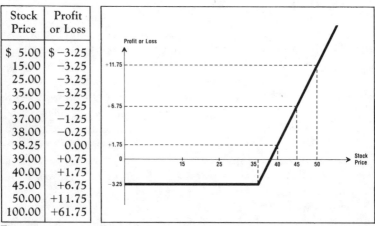

Stock Price	Profit or Loss
$ 5.00	$ −3.25
15.00	−3.25
25.00	−3.25
35.00	−3.25
36.00	−2.25
37.00	−1.25
38.00	−0.25
38.25	0.00
39.00	+0.75
40.00	+1.75
45.00	+6.75
50.00	+11.75
100.00	+61.75

Figure 1   **Figure 2**

Figures 1 and 2 are two different illustrations of the same relationship between the prices of the underlying stock and the profits or losses on the December 35 call in terms of its intrinsic value. Commissions are being ignored.

The most striking feature of this Profit/Loss Profile (or, in short, P/L Profile) is that the possible gain is unlimited while the maximum possible loss is limited by the cost of the call, i.e. $3.25 US.

I would like to stop here for a moment and say a few words for those of you who are familiar with commodity futures. Limited loss is the main difference between buying futures and buying options. The buyer of a future contract undertakes the obligation to purchase the underlying goods at a fixed price. If the price of the goods declines sharply, the owner of the future contract is still obligated to buy them at the initially fixed price. Reselling the goods in the depressed market can result in very large losses.

The owner of a call option, on the other hand, is under no obligation whatsoever. It is entirely up to him to exercise his call or not. He would exercise only if it is to his benefit.

Since the buyer of a future contract is obligated to buy the underlying goods sooner or later, he does not pay a price for the contract itself. Instead, he posts a certain sum of money as a margin or down payment, similar to the down payment on a car or a house. When the delivery is executed, the amount of margin goes toward the payment of the full price of the underlying goods.

The buyer of a call option does not undertake any obligation and, therefore, is not required to post a margin. Instead, he has to pay a price for the option. If he chooses to exercise the option later, he will also have to pay the full price of the underlying stock or commodity in addition to the price of the option which he paid earlier.

To sum up this brief discussion, the option buyer is insulated against large unfavourable moves in the underlying stock or commodity, while the buyer of a future contract is not. This additional protection costs the option buyer more money than if he bought a future contract.

A few more words about the limited risk of the option buyer. It is very important to remember that the risk is limited only by the total amount of money paid for the options. In our example of Brunswick Corp., the risk was limited by $3.25 US per share, which doesn't sound like much. However, this safety is illusive.

What if you bought 20 contracts instead of one? Even before commissions you would have paid 20 x 100 x $3.25 = $6,500.00 US. If Brunswick Corp. declined sharply and failed to recover before the end of the year, you would have lost all of the $6,500.00 US. Now that sounds more substantial than $3.25 US per share, doesn't it?

How about 200 contracts? Then you would have $65,000.00 US at risk. I don't know many people who can sleep well while having such a sum of money exposed to the possibility of a total loss. Yet it is still only $3.25 US per share!

Now you can see why I never measure risk in terms of dollars per share. I prefer staring right in the face of the entire amount paid for the options. It helps me to remember that the total sum of so many hundreds or thousands of dollars can be lost in a matter of days if the stock moves sharply against me and fails to recover before the expiry.

Yet it is good to know that you cannot lose more than you pay for options. It comes in handy before you buy options, rather than after. Since you cannot lose more than you invest, you can decide in advance how much you are prepared to risk, which is the subject of my first Rule:

Rule 1: NEVER PUT MORE MONEY INTO BUYING OPTIONS THAN YOU ARE PREPARED TO LOSE.

Once you have decided how much money you are ready to risk on a particular trade, you have to pick the right option. This, in turn, means that you must choose between different expiration months and strike prices. In order to make the best choice, you will have to develop a good forecast of the underlying stock.

Even a quick glance at the P/L Profile of a long call, illustrated in Figures 1 and 2, will tell you that to make money on a long call (i.e. a call option that you own), you would need the underlying stock to move up.

Not only that, but you would need a relatively large move. Returning to Brunswick Corp., if the stock moved up only to $37.00 US, the owner of the December 35 call purchased for $3.25 US might end up losing $1.25 US. The stock has to move above $38.25 US before the call owner would make any profit based on the intrinsic value.

So what you need is a stock ready for a sharp move up. Until you have found such a stock, you shouldn't even start thinking about buying calls. Yet many investors start the entire process from the wrong end. Quite often I receive phone calls with the following request:

"Alex, I feel like buying some calls. Which ones should I buy now?"

"What stock do you have in mind?" is my usual response.

"I don't know. That's what I am calling you for."

I take time to explain that acting on a sudden urge to buy call options is not the best approach for making money. First of all, you need a stock which you expect to move up sharply in the near future. You can use fundamental or technical analysis or a combination of both, but you absolutely need a statistically reliable forecast of the underlying stock staging a rally. Only then should you cast your first glance on the available call options.

Let us imagine that on February 2, 1984, you were watching Canadian Pacific Limited, which was trading at $45.75 Cdn. on the

Toronto Stock Exchange. Your analysis indicated that there was a high probability of the stock moving to $55.00 Cdn. You wanted to capitalize on the expected move by buying calls.

On that day, February 2, 1984, you had a choice between May 45 calls, May 50 calls, May 55 calls, August 45 calls, August 50 calls, August 55 calls, November 45 calls, November 50 calls and November 55 calls. Which one should you buy?

Looking at the prices of all those calls, you could quickly notice that the longer the life of the call, the more expensive it was. For example, November 50 calls were more expensive than August 50 calls, which in turn were more expensive than May 50 calls. Such a relationship makes sense because the longer the remaining life of the option, the more chances for the underlying stock to move up.

Since you undoubtedly know that the only way to make money is to buy cheap and sell dear, you are automatically pulled toward the May calls, because they are the cheapest. Most of the buyers do that all the time — they buy the nearest expiry because it is cheaper than others. Unfortunately, such reasoning is not much more sound than buying a used car for $100 only to discover that the engine is missing!

You don't want the cheapest option. You want to buy a call which has enough time before expiration for the underlying stock to make the expected move. When do you expect the stock to rally? This is the key question.

If you don't know the answer, you have to go back and do more work on your forecast. You cannot buy a call option and then sit and wait indefinitely for the rally. You can do that if you buy the stock itself, but not the calls. Unlike stocks, options have a nasty habit of expiring. Therefore:

IN ORDER TO MAKE MONEY IN OPTIONS, YOU MUST PAY
AS MUCH ATTENTION TO THE TIMING
OF THE EXPECTED STOCK MOVE AS TO THE DIRECTION
AND MAGNITUDE OF THIS MOVE

Let us say that you expected Canadian Pacific Limited to rally to $55.00 Cdn. in May-June 1984. Could you still buy May calls? I wouldn't. Call options are known to expire just one day before the rally in the underlying stock. It happens far more often than one would expect. Sometimes it seems that the underlying stock is sitting there waiting for the expiration day. Your calls expire on Friday, and on Monday the stock opens up a dollar and keeps moving like a ballistic rocket! It has happened to me and to every other option player I know.

When it happened to a friend of mine who didn't have a cat to kick, he ran out of the house and kicked his neighbour's Doberman. For the next month I visited him at the hospital and we carefully avoided talking about the stock market in general and options in particular. The only good thing about that incident was that the expired call was not the one I had recommended.

Rule 2: YOU SHOULD BUY ONLY THOSE OPTIONS THAT WILL EXPIRE AFTER THE TIME PERIOD DURING WHICH YOU EXPECT THE UNDERLYING STOCK TO REACH YOUR TARGET.

In the case of Canadian Pacific Limited, this Rule would force you to buy August calls, provided that all other conditions for buying calls were met. Note that the choice of the expiration month can and should be made before you even look at option prices.

Now your choice has narrowed to the following three series of calls:

August 45 calls   trading at $4.25 Cdn.,
August 50 calls   trading at $1.95 Cdn.,
August 55 calls   trading at $0.80 Cdn.

The next step is to compare the profits which would be generated by each series of calls when the underlying stock reaches your target.

When Canadian Pacific Limited trades at $55.00 Cdn., an August 45 call will have the intrinsic value of $10.00 Cdn. (To check it, consider that you could exercise the call, which means buy the stock at $45.00 Cdn., and immediately sell it for $55.00 Cdn.) Since the initial cost of an August 45 call was $4.25 Cdn., your profit before commissions would be equal to $10.00 − $4.25 = $5.75 Cdn. The percentage gain could then be calculated as follows:

$$\frac{\$5.75}{\$4.25} \times 100\% = 135\%.$$

At the same time (i.e. when Canadian Pacific Limited reached the target price of $55.00 Cdn.) an August 50 call would have the intrinsic value of $5.00 Cdn. Since its initial cost was $1.95 Cdn., the profit on this call would be equal to $5.00 − $1.95 = $3.05 Cdn. The percentage gain would be equal to

$$\frac{\$3.05}{\$1.95} \times 100\% = 156\%.$$

August 55 calls would have an intrinsic value of zero when Canadian Pacific traded at $55.00 Cdn. Consequently, instead of a profit, these calls would generate a 100% loss.

The above analysis clearly singles out August 50 calls as the most profitable. They are the ones you should buy.

Why do I use percentage gains when comparing profits on different options? The answer to this question can be found in Rule 1. That Rule requires that you decide how much money you are going to risk on any trade. Let us say that you decide to risk $1,000.00 Cdn. on Canadian Pacific Limited calls. Once this has been determined, you know exactly how many calls you can afford to buy at any given price. For example, you could buy 12 contracts of August 55 calls or 5 contracts of August 50 calls or only 2 contracts of August 45 calls, since every contract is for 100 shares.

Since you could not buy the same number of contracts in these different series, it is pointless to compare their respective profits per share. What you are interested in is which option will bring a higher profit on your $1,000.00 Cdn. investment. The answer to this question lies in their respective percentage gains.

If this is not obvious to you, I recommend that you calculate profits on $1,000.00 Cdn. and make sure that August 50 calls emerge winners.

Rule 3: WHEN BUYING OPTIONS, YOU SHOULD SELECT THE STRIKE PRICE WHICH PRODUCES THE HIGHEST GAIN PER SHARE IN PERCENTAGE TERMS WHEN THE UNDERLYING STOCK REACHES YOUR TARGET.

So far, we have established that if you were to buy Canadian Pacific Limited calls, you should have bought August calls as opposed to May or November ones, and among the August calls you should have chosen the ones with the strike price of 50. However, the main question has remained unanswered: should you really buy these calls or not? Would they be a good investment?

The answer to this question depends on what I consider to be one of the most important investment tools, the Reward/Risk Ratio. This Ratio is measured by dividing the profit you will make if your forecast comes true (the Reward) by the loss you will incur if your forecast happens to be totally wrong (the Risk).

In the case of Canadian Pacific Limited August 50 calls, if your forecast of $55.00 Cdn. is a good one, you will make at least $3.05 Cdn. per share before commissions. If the forecast is wrong and the stock remains below $50.00 Cdn., you will lose your entire investment of $1.95 Cdn. per share. Consequently, your Reward/Risk Ratio in this case is equal to

$$\frac{\$3.05}{\$1.95} \times 100\% = 156\%.$$

Is this good enough to buy the calls? — The answer is yes, but before I show you why it is so, I would like to note that in this case the Reward/Risk Ratio happened to be equal to the percentage gain per share, or in other words, to the Return On Investment. However, in the case of writing options the Reward/Risk Ratio would not be equal to the Return On Investment. Assuming that the two are always the same would lead to serious errors.

How can we evaluate a Reward/Risk Ratio? Let us step aside for a moment and take a look at the big picture. Investing in options consists of buying and selling. Over a long period of time the investor makes a series of transactions, some of which result in gains while others produce losses. The colour of the ink on the bottom line depends on the combination of two factors: the number of gains relative to the number of losses and the relative size of those gains and losses. For example, if you had as many gains as losses, but the average gain was larger than the average loss, you would end up a winner. If you had slightly more gains than losses, but the average loss was much larger than the average gain, you would have a net loss on your hands.

Of course, it would be wonderful to have a lot of large gains and just a few small losses, but this book is not about daydreaming. In real life very few stock forecasters can produce a track record of better than 65% over a long period of time. In fact, any track record better than 55% over, say, five years is an excellent achievement. Therefore, we will assume that your ability to forecast stocks is only marginally better than 50%. (Remember that if your batting average is not better than 50%, you should stay as far away as possible from options!)

This is where the Reward/Risk Ratio comes in. If you are right about the underlying stocks slightly more often than you are wrong, you need your average gain to be at least as large as your average loss. Since your losses are limited only by the amount you pay for the calls, your average rewards, or gains, should be at least equal to the price of the calls. In other words, you should be doubling your money when you are right. An important note: We cannot ignore commissions when comparing gains and losses, because in real life commissions will always be there to decrease the gains and to increase the losses. Therefore, you have to double your money *after* commissions.

Rule 4: YOUR SHOULD BUY ONLY THOSE OPTIONS WHICH
WILL DOUBLE THEIR PURCHASE PRICE
(AFTER COMMISSIONS) WHEN THE UNDERLYING STOCK
REACHES YOUR TARGET.

Applying this Rule to Canadian Pacific Limited August 50 calls, we can make the final decision to buy them. Indeed, the Reward/Risk Ratio of these calls, given the target of $55.00 Cdn., was 156% before commissions. This number is high enough to remain above 100% after commissions as well. According to Rule 4, the Reward/Risk Ratio of over 100% gives the investor a green light for purchasing the calls.

Let us briefly review all the steps in the process of making the decision to buy Canadian Pacific Limited August 50 calls. First, we analyze the stock to develop a reliable forecast. This forecast must include a specific target which is expected to be reached within a specified period of time. Second, we use Rule 1 to decide how much money we can use for purchasing options. Third, we select the expiration month according to Rule 2, i.e. in such a way that our calls would not expire before the underlying stock reaches our target. Fourth, we select the strike price as per Rule 3 in order to maximize the possible gain. Fifth, we check if the Reward/Risk Ratio is greater than 100% as required by Rule 4.

Since most of the option investors buy calls as soon as they "like the stock" and never consider all the above-mentioned factors, is it any wonder that they end up losers?

However, even after you have diligently complied with Rules 1-4, you are still far away from winning the battle. In fact, you are not even half way there!

Anyone who has had sufficient experience in the stock market knows that to buy the right stuff at the right time is much easier than to sell it at the right time. The reason for that lies in human psychology.

When you are considering the purchase of an investment, it is not very difficult to be rational. You can spend a long time studying the situation and weighing pros and cons. You can consult with other people, with books, and with any other sources you consider important. You can always postpone the decision and give it more time to brew in your head. As long as your money is safely tucked away in a bank account, you are under no pressure. The worst that can happen is that while you were thinking and considering, the situation has changed and you have missed your opportunity. It hurts, but the fact that your money is intact in the bank serves as a great consolation.

Once you have made a purchase, however, the situation changes quite drastically. Now your money is on the line and every move in the wrong direction threatens you with a loss. Not only that, but moves in the right direction also affect your nervous system by tempting you to take a small profit rather than risk a reversal and a loss. All of a sudden you find yourself constantly making the decision to sell or not to sell. This puts a terrible strain on your thinking mechanism and its efficiency drops faster than any stock. Eventually, you become totally helpless in the face of two overpowering emotions, fear and greed, and you let them make the decision for you. And you can be sure of one thing — your greatest enemy couldn't make a worse decision than you will make under the influence of fear and greed.

How can you avoid that nightmare? There is only one way. You must make your selling decision *before* you make the purchase. To make this decision intelligently you need some rules for selling.

Let us begin with the most simple aspect of selling options. Once you have made the decision to close a long position in calls, should you sell them or exercise?

If you exercise calls, you can never receive more than their intrinsic value. Even that amount will be reduced by the commissions you will have to pay on buying the stock (through exercise of calls) and on selling it in the market. These commissions will always be much higher than the commission on selling the calls.

Earlier in this chapter we found out that the market price of call options cannot fall far below their intrinsic value. If we take commissions into consideration, you will always receive more money by selling your calls than by exercising them.

Rule 5: SELLING THE OPTIONS YOU OWN IS ALWAYS BETTER THAN EXERCISING THEM AND THEN CLOSING THE RESULTING POSITION IN THE UNDERLYING STOCK.

Now that we have disposed of the uncertainty as to *how* to sell, we must address a much more important and less simple question of *when* to sell.

On the surface the answer appears to be obvious. If we have established a definite target when we bought the calls, we should sell them as soon as this target is reached.

Rule 6: SELL THE OPTIONS YOU OWN AS SOON AS THE UNDERLYING STOCK HAS REACHED YOUR TARGET.

Unfortunately, this is easier said than done. When the underlying stock reaches your target, you will be strongly tempted to review the target and to try to squeeze a few more points out of the stock. Resist that temptation.

You must always remember that your original forecast which produced the first target was based on detailed analysis of objective facts. Not only that, but the analysis was done before you invested the funds and, therefore, was much more objective than anything you may come up with when you have an actual position. It is true that sometimes the circumstances might change and some new information might appear that would suggest a higher target. In most cases, however, the higher targets are a direct result of investors' greed. Even when new information is present, I would question the ability of an investor with an existing option position to analyze that information objectively.

Consequently, I recommend sticking with the original target in most cases. Upgrading your targets should be a very rare exception, rather than a rule. Sudden changes in strategy are a powerful weapon in football, boxing, or chess, but they usually bring disastrous results in investing. Many wise investors believe that a bad but consistent strategy is better than an excellent but inconsistent one. I wouldn't go that far, but it has been my experience that discipline and consistency are as important as the strategy itself.

Have we solved the problem of when to sell? Far from it! So far we have looked only at the best possible case, when the underlying stock does exactly what we expected it to do, i.e. reach our target. If our forecasts are good, our stocks will do that more than half of the time, but what should we do when our forecast does not seem to work?

One popular strategy is to sell your option position as soon as it has lost 50% of the original value. I have tried that. The results were less than satisfacory. What happened was that the underlying stock would start moving against me and the calls would lose that 50% of the purchase price with amazing ease and speed. I would sell out at a loss only to see the stock turn around and head straight to my target. Needless to say, it didn't make me happy.

From then on I have been holding my options till the very end. After all, every option position involves the amount of capital I am fully prepared to lose if my forecast is incorrect (Rule 1). Furthermore, it is difficult enough to forecast the direction, the magnitude, and the approximate timing of a stock move as it is. To expect the stock to start moving in the right direction immediately after the purchase of options is totally unrealistic. Yet a fairly small move in the opposite direction usually results in quick declines in option prices.

My policy is to ignore the option prices altogether, once I have established the position. I prefer to watch the underlying stock and to ask myself how probable it is that the stock will reach my target in time, rather than to watch the options themselves. Investors who watch options on a daily or even hourly basis can often be spotted by their shaking hands, dark circles under the eyes, the colour (silver-grey) and the amount (very little) of the hair. No, I would rather watch stocks and give them every opportunity to reach my targets.

Rule 7: DO NOT SELL THE OPTIONS YOU OWN AT A LOSS EARLIER THAN ON THE EXPIRATION DAY, UNLESS YOUR FORECAST OF THE UNDERLYING STOCK HAS CHANGED.

The condition at the end of Rule 8 is essential. One of the greatest laws of nature is that nothing remains the same for long. Things change constantly. On the previous pages, I suggested that you should be extremely cautious when dealing with positive changes. Your interpretation of such changes might be influenced by greed, which may easily result in moving your original targets to unreasonable levels.

Negative changes in the factors involved in your original forecast, however, must be dealt with as soon as they arise. It is these changes that are mentioned in Rule 7. Imagine receiving some information which makes it very questionable if the underlying stock would reach your target in time. What should you do? On the one hand, if your forecast fails you can easily lose your entire investment in the option position. This thought would undoubtedly push you toward selling the calls and salvaging whatever you can. On the other hand, neither the original forecast, nor your interpretations of the new information, are perfect. Despite all the negative factors, there is always a chance that an unexpected rally might give you a good chance to sell the calls and get *most* of your money back.

Here is what I do in such situations. As soon as new information makes me question my initial stock forecast, I look at the market price of my calls. If the price is such that I can sell and get back more than half of the initial investment, I do it right away. If I cannot get half of my money back, I leave the position open. After all, I was fully prepared to lose every penny invested in the option originally (Rule 1). And there is always a chance that a rally might just give me more than half of my money back. If such a rally materializes during the life of the calls, I sell and get my 50% plus back.

Rule 8: IF YOU BOUGHT OPTIONS AND THEN YOUR FORECAST OF THE UNDERLYING STOCK HAS CHANGED FOR

THE WORSE, SELL THE OPTIONS ONLY WHEN YOU CAN GET
50% OR MORE OF THE PURCHASE PRICE BACK (AFTER
COMMISSIONS). IF YOU CANNOT DO THAT, SELL THE
OPTIONS ON THE EXPIRATION DAY.

This Rule completes the analysis of buying calls as a bullish
strategy. Now you know how to select the calls (Rules 2, 3, and 4),
how much to invest (Rule 1), when to sell them (Rules 6, 7, and 8),
and how to sell (Rule 5). We will talk some more about the size of
your investment in options in Chapter 10.

The next section will examine the second recommended bullish
strategy — writing puts.

2. Writing Puts

Buying calls is a simple and effective strategy for using options
when you are bullish on the underlying stock. Why then should you
even bother to look at other bullish strategies? As you will find out,
following all the Rules for buying calls makes you quite selective.
Very often you will not find any calls on the stock you like that would
satisfy all the requirements. It is in such cases that you should
investigate the strategy of writing puts.

Imagine that on February 6, 1984, you were bullish on Alcan.
The stock was trading at $42.00 Cdn. on the Toronto Stock Ex-
change. Your analysis indicated that the stock should reach $48.00
Cdn. within 4-5 months. Your first thought was, of course, to buy
some calls. Following Rule 2, you chose August calls. On February 6,
1984, you had to pay the following prices for August calls on Alcan:

$5.00 Cdn. for August 40 calls,
$2.75 Cdn. for August 45 calls,
$1.35 Cdn. for August 50 calls.

The next step was to check if any of those calls satisfied Rule 4.
Unfortunately, the answer was negative. None of the above calls
would double its purchase price if Alcan reached your target of
$48.00 Cdn. just before expiration. Therefore, buying calls was not a
good idea.

That was the time for you to look at the puts.

Let us take a close look at August 40 puts, which at that time were
trading at $2.00 Cdn. If you bought such a put, it would give you the
right to sell Alcan at $40.00 Cdn. at any time before expiration.
Since you expected the stock to rally to $48.00 Cdn., selling at
$40.00 Cdn. would make very little sense indeed!

So buying these puts wasn't a good idea either. What about

writing them? If you wrote an Alcan August 40 put, you would have undertaken the obligation to buy the stock at $40.00 Cdn. Had you been forced to honour the obligation you could then sell the stock at $48.00 Cdn. when your target was reached. The end result would be a nice profit.

Since this sounds much better than buying the same put, let us examine the possible consequences of writing an August 40 put on Alcan in greater detail.

If the puts were exercised, you would own Alcan at $40.00 Cdn. If the stock then ran up to your target of $48.00 Cdn., you would sell it and make $8.00 Cdn. on the stock alone (before commissions). In addition to that, you would keep the $2.00 Cdn. that you received for writing the puts in the first place. That would increase your profit to $8.00 + $2.00 = $10.00 Cdn. before commissions.

Unfortunately, you have no control over the puts you write, it is not up to you to exercise them or not. This is entirely in the hands of the owner of those puts. What if the puts were not exercised and Alcan ran up to your target of $48.00 Cdn.? In that case you would end up keeping the $2.00 Cdn. that you received for writing the put. It is much less attractive than the $10.00 Cdn. profit you would have made had the put been exercised but, nevertheless, it is a profit.

As you can see, even if the underlying stock reaches your target, your profit as a put writer depends on the actions of the put owner. Therefore:

ALL THE STRATEGIES RELATED TO WRITING OPTIONS MUST BE ANALYZED FIRST FROM THE STANDPOINT OF THE OPTION BUYER, SINCE IT IS THE BUYER WHO DETERMINES IF THE OPTION IS GOING TO BE EXERCISED.

Returning to the Alcan August 40 put that you wrote, it would not make any sense for the owner of that put to exercise it as long as Alcan trades above $40.00 Cdn. Indeed, if the market price is above $40.00 Cdn., why would the owner of the put want to sell the stock for $40.00 Cdn.?

Consequently, if Alcan stays above $40.00 Cdn. until the expiration of the put, you will keep the $2.00 Cdn. that you received when you wrote the put.

What if Alcan falls to, say, $35.00 Cdn.? In this case, the owner of the put will probably exercise it. By exercising the put he would sell Alcan for $40.00 Cdn. which is much better than selling it at the market price of $35.00 Cdn. Obviously, the owner would do it if he had the stock. But even if he didn't, it would still make sense for him to exercise the put, which would make him short Alcan at $40.00 Cdn. He could then immediately buy the stock in the market at $35.00 Cdn., making a profit of $5.00 Cdn. on the stock.

When the put is exercised, you will be forced to buy the stock at $40.00 Cdn. Since you were not interested in keeping the stock, you would then have to close the position by selling Alcan in the market for $35.00 Cdn. This would result in a loss of $5.00 Cdn. on the stock. The loss would be reduced, of course, by the $2.00 Cdn. that you received for the put at the very beginning. Your net loss (before commissions) would be equal to $5.00 − $2.00 = $3.00 Cdn.

Repeating similar calculations for various prices of Alcan, we can fill up the table presented in Figure 3 or draw a graph presented in Figure 4. Both the table and the graph illustrate the Profit/Loss Profile of a put writer.

Stock Price	Profit or Loss
$ 5.00	$ −33.00
15.00	−23.00
25.00	−13.00
35.00	−3.00
36.00	−2.00
37.00	−1.00
38.00	−0.00
39.00	+1.00
40.00	+2.00
45.00	+2.00
55.00	+2.00
100.00	+2.00

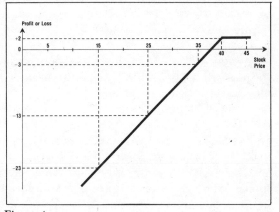

Figure 3   Figure 4

As you can see, this Profit/Loss Profile is drastically different from that of a call owner (see Figures 1 and 2). The only similarity lies in the fact that both the call buyer and the put writer make money when the underlying stock goes up and lose money when the underlying stock goes down. In other words, both strategies are bullish. And this is where the similarity ends.

While the call buyer enjoys limited risk and unlimited potential gain, the put writer should not expect to make more than what he received for the put. As far as the put writer's risk is concerned, even though it is limited, it can be many times larger than the potential gain.

Given these differences in the Profit/Loss Profile, it is obvious that an investor bullish on the underlying stock should always explore the possibility of buying calls. Only when he finds out that no calls satisfy all the pertinent Rules, should he turn his attention to writing puts.

One interesting feature of the Profit/Loss Profile of a put writer is that the writer makes his maximum profit as long as the puts stay out-of-the-money. When the puts are out-of-the-money, the owner will not exercise them, and the writer will get to keep the original payment for the puts.

This means that the writer is not really concerned with a precise forecast for the underlying stock. He doesn't care if the stock stages a strong rally or not, and if it does he doesn't care when. All the writer needs is for the stock to remain above the strike price, or in other words, for the puts to remain out-of-the-money.

Such being the case, it is obvious that one should never write puts that are already in-the-money at the time of writing. Doing that, one would risk the puts being exercised immediately, which would force one to buy the stock back and to pay commissions on both selling and buying the stock. These commissions will bite a large chunk off the writer's profit.

When writing out-of-the-money puts, you are guaranteed that the puts will not be exercised as long as the underlying stock does not move against you, i.e. down.

Another important consideration is that you should try to write the puts that have a decent price. The reason is that your maximum profit is equal to the amount you receive for the puts. It obviously makes very little sense to write the cheapest puts around! Since puts get cheaper as they move farther away from being at-the-money, you should write those that are as close as possible to being at-the-money in order to maximize the price you receive for them.

Rule 9: WRITE ONLY OUT-OF-THE-MONEY OPTIONS WHICH ARE THE CLOSEST TO BEING AT-THE-MONEY.

This Rule helps you to select the best strike price for writing puts. The question of selecting the appropriate expiration month is still open. When we discussed buying calls, the lifetime of the calls had to be closely linked to the timing of the expected rally in the stock. As we have already discussed, the writer of puts in not as concerned with the timing of the stock move as the buyer of the calls. All the writer of puts really cares about is that the stock should stay above the strike price during the life of the puts. This allows the put writer more freedom in selecting the expiration month.

As we have already discussed, option premiums, be it calls or puts, are the highest when the option has full nine months before expiry. The closer the time gets to the expiry, the less time there is for the underlying stock to move up (in the case of calls) or down (in the case of puts), and the lower drop the prices that buyers pay for them.

Consequently, it makes no sense for the writer to write the options that are about to expire. The prices of such options offer very little profit potential. If the writer's only objective was to maximize the price received for the put, he should write the one with the longest life. Such tactics, however, leave too much time for the underlying stock to move against the writer. The best solution lies in between:

Rule 10: WRITE ONLY THOSE OPTIONS WHICH HAVE BETWEEN 2 AND 5 MONTHS UNTIL EXPIRATION.

Even combining Rules 9 and 10 will not guarantee that the price of the put you are about to write is worth the trouble. The last step before writing a put is to take a close look at the price of the put itself:

Rule 11: WRITE ONLY THOSE OPTIONS WHOSE PRICE IS AT LEAST 10% OF THE STRIKE PRICE.

Now you have all the ammunition you need to write the puts that will maximize your chances for winning. Yet in all the discussion of the Rules for writing puts, we have not addressed the unfavourable Reward/Risk Ratio of a put writer.

I hope you remember our discussion of the Reward/Risk Ratio in relation to buying calls. If not, I strongly recommend you go back and read that section again. In that discussion we came to the conclusion that in order to be a winner in the long run, the investor must make sure that the Reward/Risk Ratio of all his positions was not less than 100%. In other words, your gain when you are right should not be smaller than your loss when you are wrong. Rule 4 provided specific instructions for maintaining the required Reward/Risk Ratio when buying calls.

One look at Figures 3 and 4 will be sufficient for you to see that the Reward/Risk Ratio of a put writer is the exact opposite of what you would like it to be. Simply stated, the rewards are small and the risks are high.

This is why a put writer must undertake additional steps to create a favourable Reward/Risk Ratio. This is done by using stop-losses.

I have tried placing stop-losses on the prices of the options themselves, but the results were disappointing. Very often option prices leaped over my stop-losses without triggering them. In addition, several Option Exchanges refused to accept stop-losses on options altogether.

A much better way is to place *a mental stop-loss* on the price of the underlying stock. A *mental stop-loss* is the price of the underlying stock which serves as a signal to close the option position. As soon as the stock reaches your mental stop-loss, you buy back the puts that you have written before.

Let us return to the example of Alcan August 40 puts. If you decided to write those puts, your profit potential would be $2.00 Cdn., since such was the price you could receive for the puts. To maintain the Reward/Risk Ratio of not less than 100% you would have to limit your possible loss by $2.00 Cdn. The technique I use is to close the option position as soon as the underlying stock has moved against me to the extent of the amount I have received for the option.

Since on February 6, 1984, when you were writing the August 40 puts, Alcan was trading at $42.00 Cdn., I would place my mental stop-loss at $42.00 − $2.00 = $40.00 Cdn. In other words, having written the puts for $2.00 Cdn., I would buy them back as soon as the underlying stock declined by $2.00 Cdn.

If Alcan declined from $42.00 Cdn. to $40.00 Cdn., the price of the August 40 puts would rise from $2.00 Cdn. to a higher number. In most cases, however, the price of puts rises more slowly in terms of dollars per share than the price of the underlying stock declines. As a result, when Alcan reached $40.00 Cdn., you would buy back your August 40 puts for less than $4.00 Cdn. Your loss, therefore, would be smaller than $2.00 Cdn.

Later in this chapter I will show that it is not prudent to wait until expiration after you have written a put. I will recommend taking your profits earlier by buying the puts back. Consequently, you will not be able to obtain the maximum possible gain. My stop-loss Rule will help you to match the risk with the reward in such a way as to keep the Reward/Risk Ratio larger than 100% on the average.

Rule 12: WHEN WRITING PUTS, PLACE A MENTAL STOP-LOSS AT THE PRICE WHICH IS EQUAL TO THE PRICE OF THE UNDERLYING STOCK AT THE TIME OF WRITING MINUS THE PRICE OF THE PUT.

As good as this Rule is, it is not foolproof. In our example, if there was an unexpected announcement about Alcan, when it was trading at, say, $41.00 Cdn., the trading could be stopped for a while. If trading resumed later at a price of $38.00 Cdn., you would have to buy back the put at whatever price existed in the market. It could very well be higher than $4.00 Cdn.

Fortunately, such extraordinary events happen very rarely. And the better your forecasts of the underlying stocks, the less often these bad surprises will harm you. In the long run, the multitude of smaller gains on writing options will produce more than enough profits to cover a few larger losses.

Now that you know all there is to know about when and how to write puts, the next question is, when and how to take profits?

Option writers are usually inclined to sit and wait until expiry in order to retain the full price received for the option at the time of writing. My experience shows that it is not the best approach.

Let us say you wrote some puts and the underlying stock started moving up soon after that. Watching put prices, you will notice that at the beginning they will be declining quite rapidly. However, as the stock moves further and further away from the strike price, the changes in the price of the option slow down. It may take only three weeks for a put to decline from $2.00 to $0.50, but it might well require four months before it drops from $0.50 to $0.05, while the underlying stock continues to climb. The cheaper the option, the slower the rate of decline of its price.

Since you make most of your gain as soon as the underlying stock moves up, it is not worth your while to wait until expiration. First, you are not going to increase your gain by much. Second, there is always a chance that the stock will drop suddenly and you will end up with a loss instead of a profit.

Rule 13: COVER YOUR SHORT POSITIONS AS SOON AS YOU CAN MAKE A PROFIT (AFTER COMMISSIONS) EQUAL TO 75% OF THE INITIAL PRICE OF THE OPTION.

The above Rule should be used when everything goes according to the plan, which means that the underlying stock remains above the strike price and you expect it to stay there. Unfortunately, sometimes things change right in the middle of the show. We do all the hard work forecasting the stock and selecting the best option, we take our position — and then bang! — there is news that changes our forecast and threatens to rob us of our carefully planned out profit. What to do?

The most important thing is to fight the impulse to hope for the best. Wishful thinking is the main reason for investment losses. If you want to be a winner, you absolutely have to conquer this popular trait!

Go back to Figures 3 and 4 and look at them very carefully. Concentrate on the size of the possible losses. That is what you are faced with when the forecast of the underlying stock turns sour. Once you have fully realized that, it will become crystal clear to you that when something like that happens, you should cut your losses and run for your life!

Rule 14: IF YOUR FORECAST OF THE UNDERLYING STOCK HAS CHANGED UNFAVOURABLY, CLOSE ALL SHORT POSITIONS IMMEDIATELY.

If you follow all the above Rules, the puts you write will seldom be exercised. Most of the time you would be buying them back at a profit or loss. Profits will show up more often than losses and you will be accumulating net profits.

Yet from time to time the puts you wrote would still be exercised. What should you do then?

You should fight the temptation to keep the stock. Remember, you wrote the puts in order to buy them back at a lower price. You did not want to own the stock. Writing puts in order to buy the underlying stock is a different strategy, and we will analyze it in Chapter 9. Since you didn't want to own the stock when you wrote the puts, you should not change your mind in the middle of the game. We have already discussed the danger of changing your strategy half-way. Therefore, you should simply sell the stock and thus close the long position which arose after the puts were exercised.

But the temptation will be strong. Imagine that on December 9, 1983 you wrote a July 30 put on Goodyear Tire and received $2.12 US for it. At that time the stock was trading at $30.50 US and looked as if it was ready to go higher. Instead, by December 16, 1983 Goodyear Tire declined to $29.38 US, while your put rose to $2.50 US. According to Rule 12, your mental stop-loss was set at $30.50 − $2.12 = $28.38 US. Since the stock was trading above your stop-loss, you were prepared to wait.

Unfortunately, you were not allowed to wait. The put was exercised and you found yourself buying the stock at $30.00 US. As you reached for the phone to call your broker and to instruct him to sell the stock, a soft, sweet voice whispered in your ear: "Don't sell. Wait a little. The stock looks good. Now that you own it you can make a lot of money. If it runs up to $40.00 US, you will sell it for a $10.00 US gain plus the $2.12 US you received for the put. Your total profit will be equal to $10.00 + $2.12 = $12.12 US which is much more than what you were shooting for in the first place. Just keep the stock a while longer!"

This is where you need all your will power. The sweet little voice will lead you straight to the poor house if you give in. What you should do is ask this tempting voice a simple question: What if the stock continues to decline? One look at the Profit/Loss Profile of a put writer should be sufficient to send chills down your spine. In my experience, this simple question, supported by reference to the Profit/Loss Profile is more than sufficient to silence the soft, sweet voice of temptation.

One more important point: even though you know that your forecasts are not perfect, you nevertheless, do your best to make sure that the stock is likely to go up rather than down before you write a put. Therefore, when the stock does move down, you should increase the level of caution and scepticism with regard to your forecast. It is possible that the decline is only temporary and the expected rally will follow later, but it is also possible that you missed something in your analysis. Whenever a stock goes against me, I question the validity of my forecast. It does not mean that I close the position before my stop-loss has been touched, but I do not increase the size of my position by averaging down and I do not keep the stock position if the puts are exercised.

Rule 15: IF YOU WROTE OPTIONS WITH THE INTENTION OF BUYING THEM BACK LATER AND THEY WERE EXERCISED, IMMEDIATELY CLOSE THE RESULTING STOCK POSITION.

Actually, you should be quite happy when the puts you have written are exercised. Let us return to the example of Goodyear Tire. When the puts were exercised, you found yourself an owner of the stock at $30.00 US. Following Rule 15, you imediately sold it at the market price of $29.38 US. As a result, you lost $30.00 − $29.38 = $0.62 US on the stock, but you kept the $2.12 US received for the put. Even after commissions you would end up a winner. If the puts were not exercised and the stock declined further, your stop-loss would have been triggered and you would have bought the put back at a loss.

The last question related to writing puts has to do with cash management. How many puts should you write?

In the case of buying calls, the answer was simple. All you had to do was to take the total amount of dollars you were prepared to risk on that particular trade and divide it by the price of one call contract.

Since you are not paying anything when writing puts, but instead you are receiving some cash, the situation is somewhat more complicated. Of course, your broker will require that you post a margin against possible losses, but the amount of margin is not related to the Reward/Risk Ratio of your position and, therefore, cannot be used in calculating the number of put contracts you can afford to write.

The Rule I use is based on the mental stop-loss determined by

Rule 12. Since we place a mental stop-loss that will allow the underlying stock to move against us by as many dollars as we have received for the puts, I assume that we can lose that much (even though usually the loss on puts will be smaller). If we accept that assumption, the situation becomes very similar to the one of buying calls. All we have to do is take the total amount we are prepared to risk and divide it by the price of one put contract.

Rule 16: WHEN WRITING UNCOVERED OPTIONS, THE AMOUNT OF MONEY YOU RECEIVE SHOULD NOT EXCEED THE AMOUNT OF MONEY YOU ARE PREPARED TO LOSE.

Let us illustrate this Rule on the example of Goodyear Tire. The puts you were about to write were worth $2.12 US per share. Following Rule 12, you placed a mental stop-loss $2.12 US below the market price of the stock at the time of writing. In other words, you were prepared to wait for as long as the stock declined less that $2.12 US. If and when that happened, you were going to buy the puts back at a loss. How big would that loss be?

It is impossible to tell for sure, but we know that the put would not grow dollar-for-dollar when the stock declined. Therefore, when Goodyear Tire declined by $2.12 US, your July 30 put would have grown *less* than $2.12 US. Since we don't know how much less, we will assume the worst, i.e. that it would decline by $2.12 US. This is, therefore, the amount of your risk calculated on a per share basis.

If you were prepared to risk, say, $2,000.00 US on this position, you would divide $2,000.00 by $212.00, which is the price of one contract (since there are 100 shares in one contract). You could afford to write 9 puts.

This completes the chapter devoted to recommended bullish option strategies. From time to time, you will find yourself in a situation where you are bullish on the underlying stock, but you can neither buy calls nor write puts without violating some of the Rules set out in this chapter. What should you do then?

My advice is: Keep it simple, buy the stock!

Options can be a very profitable investment vehicle. But to make them work for you, you should not use them indiscriminately. Rather, you should capitalize on exceptional opportunities they present from time to time. My Rules are designed to highlight such opportunities and to help you make the most of them.

Chapter 6

Recommended Strategies — Bearish
1. Buying Puts
2. Writing Calls

After having read the previous chapter, you have probably guessed that my favourite bearish strategies are buying puts and writing naked calls. Of course, buying puts is my first choice because the possible losses are limited by the amount invested, while the possible gains are quite large compared with the losses. When puts are too expensive to buy, however, the second best course of action is to write naked calls. As you will see, the writer of naked calls must take even more precautions than the writer of puts, but nevertheless it is a valid and potentially profitable strategy. I dislike bearish spreads as much as bullish ones, the reasons for which are presented in Chapter 9.

Throughout the whole discussion of buying puts and writing calls in this chapter, I will assume that the investor does not own the underlying stock or have a short position in it. Buying puts against a long position in the underlying stock is a separate strategy which is analyzed in Chapter 8.

1. Buying Puts

Buying puts is very similar to buying calls. The only difference is in the direction of the expected move in the underlying stock. While the call buyer expects the underlying stock to go up, the put buyer banks on a decline. Even though this difference is not very significant, it bears one implication that is often overlooked. When stock prices rise, there is no limit to how far they can go. In a strong bull market most stocks will double, while some will triple and even quadruple in price. Such is not the case in a bear market. No stock can possibly lose more than 100% of its value. In fact, in a severe bear market the majority of stocks will depreciate 60-70% and the worst performers will lose 100% by going bankrupt.

A good example is Coleco. During the period from November, 1981 to June, 1983, its shares soared from $3.10 US to $64.00 US. Measured in percentage terms, the gain amounted to 1,965% ! If you bought Coleco at $3.10 US on a 50% margin in November, 1981, $3,200.00 US would have bought you 2,000 shares. Having sold these shares for $64.00 US in June, 1983, you would have received $128,000.00 US. Your gain in dollar terms would have been $124,800.00 US.

On the other hand, if you shorted Coleco in June, 1983 at the price of $64.00 US and if you used the same 50% margin and the same initial capital of $3,200.00 US, you would have been able to sell short only 100 shares (ignoring commissions). Were Coleco to decline back to $3.10 US, you would have bought the 100 shares back at that price. Your profit would have amounted to

$$(\$64.00 - \$3.10) \times 100 = \$6,090.00 \text{ US},$$

which is not bad at all, but certainly cannot be compared to the $124,800.00 US made on the upside.

As you can see, it is much easier to make money on the upside than on the downside, even though many traders and brokers claim the opposite. What are the implications for a put buyer?

Since the potential gains on the downside are much smaller than those on the upside, the owner of puts must be prepared to take profits faster than the owner of calls.

Rule 17: A PUT OWNER SHOULD NEVER MOVE DOWN HIS ORIGINAL TARGET FOR THE UNDERLYING STOCK. THE PROFIT SHOULD BE TAKEN AS SOON AS THE ORIGINAL TARGET IS REACHED.

From here on, our analysis of buying puts will closely parallel that of buying calls. As in the case of calls, the future prices of puts cannot be calculated in advance. Therefore, we will use the intrinsic values of puts as conservative estimates of the prices. Also, we will ignore commissions, which differ depending on the option prices and the number of contracts being traded.

Before we go any further, I would like to remind you of the most important discovery presented in Chapter 4:

IT IS THE MOVEMENT OF THE UNDERLYING STOCK THAT CREATES PROFITS OR LOSSES ON OPTIONS.

Such being the case, our next logical step is to analyze the influence of the movement of the underlying stock on the profits or losses generated by a long put position. In other words, we are going to build the Profit/Loss Profile of a put buyer.

Imagine that on January 9, 1983, you bought Dome Mines July 15 put at $1.50 Cdn. On that day Dome Mines was trading at $16.00 Cdn. What would happen if the stock rallied to $20.00 Cdn.?

The put you owned gave you the right to sell 100 shares of Dome Mines at $15.00 Cdn. I would like to remind you that you did not own the stock itself. It would do you no good exercising the put and finding yourself short 100 shares of Dome Mines at $15.00 Cdn., when the market price of the stock was $20.00 Cdn. In other words, your put was worthless. At that time the $1.50 Cdn. paid for the put was the exact amount of your loss. (Of course, you might have been able to sell the put to someone for 10¢ or 5¢, but we cannot rely on such a possibiity in our analysis.)

The argument presented above would hold true for any price of Dome Mines above $15.00 Cdn.

Let us turn now to the brighter side. What if Dome Mines fell to $10.00 Cdn.? That would change the situation, wouldn't it? Now you would be more than happy to exercise the put and become short 100 shares of Dome Mines at $15.00 Cdn., because you would then immediately turn around and buy the shares back in the market at $10.00 Cdn. Your profit on the stock would amount to $15.00 − $10.00 = $5.00 Cdn. After deducting the $1.50 Cdn. paid for the put, you would arrive at the net profit of $3.50 Cdn. It is entirely possible that you could sell the put itself for a price better than $5.00 Cdn. instead of exercising it, but since such an opportunity cannot be predicted with any degree of accuracy, we will use the intrinsic value of $5.00 Cdn. for our calculations.

Analyzing potential profits and losses at other prices of Dome Mines, you can easily fill the table or plot the graph on Figure 6.

As you can see, the Profit/Loss Potential of a put buyer is very similar to that of a call buyer (see Figures 1 and 2). The main difference is that the put buyer makes money when the underlying stock declines, while the call buyer makes money when the underlying stock rises. This is why buying puts is a bearish strategy.

Another difference is that the potential gain of a put buyer, even though much greater than the potential loss, is still limited. The limitation stems from the fact that the underlying stock cannot decline below zero.

Let us compare, for a minute, the position of a put buyer with that of a seller of a future contract. The main advantage of the put buyer is his limited risk. The seller of a future contract undertakes the

Stock Price	Profit or Loss
$ 1.00	$ +12.50
5.00	+8.50
10.00	+3.50
11.00	+2.50
12.00	+1.50
13.00	+0.50
13.50	0.00
14.00	−0.50
15.00	−1.50
16.00	−1.50
20.00	−1.50
50.00	−1.50
100.00	−1.50

Figure 5

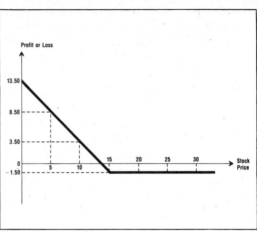

Figure 6

obligation to sell the underlying commodity or security in the future. If that commodity or security rises in price, the seller of the future contract will sustain a loss. The stronger the rally in the commodity or security, the greater the loss. In fact, such losses are unlimited!

The basic law of Nature, however, states that there is no free lunch. The seller of a future contract undertakes an obligation that he is going to fulfil. Consequently, the "margin" posted with the broker or Exchange is treated as a downpayment. It becomes a part of the amount required to settle the sale of the underlying commodity or security.

A put buyer, who is under no obligation, pays the price of the put with the full understanding that he will never see that money again. If he decides to exercise his put later, the price of the put does not enter into the calculation of how much he receives from the sale of the underlying commodity or security. In short, the put buyer pays for the privilege of having his risk limited.

In Chapter 5, we discussed the limited risk feature of a call buyer. We discovered that even though it sounds very safe to be risking "only" so many dollars per share, in actual fact the risk was limited by the amount of the total investment. The same applies to puts. You cannot lose more than you pay for them, but of that amount you can lose every penny!

This is why I formulated Rule 1 using the word "options" instead of the word "calls." The rule applies equally to calls and puts:

Rule 1: NEVER PUT MORE MONEY INTO BUYING OPTIONS THAN YOU ARE PREPARED TO LOSE.

Actually, most of the Rules applicable to calls are also applicable to puts. That is why I have formulated them in terms of "options" rather than "calls." We will review these Rules here briefly, but if you feel the need for a more detailed analysis, I recommend going back to Chapter 5. Select your own examples of put options and repeat all the analytical steps presented in Chapter 5. Take as many examples as you need to make the logistics and the conclusions perfectly clear.

Rule 2 deals with the selection of the most appropriate expiration month. As in the case of calls, a put buyer does not want to pay too much for his option, but he absolutely must have enough time for the underlying stock to make the expected move:

Rule 2: YOU SHOULD BUY ONLY THOSE OPTIONS WHICH WILL EXPIRE AFTER THE TIME PERIOD DURING WHICH YOU EXPECT THE UNDERLYING STOCK TO REACH YOUR TARGET.

Once you have selected the expiration month according to Rule 2, you should pick the best put on the basis of the expected percentage gain:

Rule 3: WHEN BUYING OPTIONS, YOU SHOULD SELECT THE STRIKE PRICE WHICH PRODUCES THE HIGHEST GAIN PER SHARE IN PERCENTAGE TERMS WHEN THE UNDERLYING STOCK REACHES YOUR TARGET.

For example, if you were bearish on Inco and expected it to decline from $17.25 Cdn. on February 2, 1984 to $14.00 Cdn. sometime before the end of July, 1984, you were probably thinking of buying some August puts. On February 2, 1984, you had a choice among the following put options:

August 15 puts,	trading at $0.60 Cdn.,
August 17½ puts,	trading at $1.30 Cdn.,
August 20 puts,	trading at $3.00 Cdn.

If Inco indeed fell to $14.00 Cdn., the intrinsic value of August 15 puts would become $1.00 Cdn. To check it, imagine that you exercised the puts, became short the stock at $15.00 Cdn., and then covered the stock position by buying the shares back in the market at $14.00 Cdn. Your gain on the stock of $15.00 − $14.00 = $1.00 Cdn. would be equal to the intrinsic value of these puts by definition. Deducting the original price of $0.60 Cdn. from the intrinsic value of

$1.00 Cdn., you would end up with a net profit of $0.40 Cdn. Your percentage gain would then be equal to:

$$\frac{\$0.40}{\$0.60} \times 100\% = 67\%.$$

At the same price of $14.00 Cdn. for the underlying stock, the intrinsic value of August 17½ calls would be equal to $17.50 − $14.00 = $3.50 Cdn. The net profit in percentage terms could then be calculated as follows:

$$\frac{\$3.50 - \$1.30}{\$1.30} \times 100\% = 169\%.$$

August 20 puts would have the intrinsic value of $20.00 − $14.00 = $6.00 Cdn., when Inco traded at the target price of $14.00 Cdn. The net profit in percentage terms for these puts would be equal to:

$$\frac{\$6.00 - \$3.00}{\$3.00} \times 100\% = 100\%.$$

Obviously, the best buy would be August 17½ puts, since they would deliver the highest profit in percentage terms when the underlying stock reached its target.

Should you then go ahead and buy these puts? Not yet. First you have to check if the Reward/Risk Ratio is on your side. Here, as well, the puts are no different from calls. Since you hope to have more gains then losses, but not by a very large margin, you should try to keep the Reward/Risk Ratio on the greater side of 100%, as explained in Chapter 5. In other words, you must follow Rule 4:

Rule 4: YOU SHOULD BUY ONLY THOSE OPTIONS WHICH
WILL DOUBLE THEIR PURCHASE PRICE
(AFTER COMMISSIONS) WHEN THE UNDERLYING STOCK
REACHES YOUR TARGET.

Inco August 17½ calls satisfy this condition as well. The profit of 169% before commissions is large enough to cover the commissions and still remain above 100%. In a real life situation you can calculate the commissions precisely, because you know exactly how many contracts you are going to buy. You can always obtain the commission table from your broker.

Not only are the Rules for buying puts very similar to those for buying calls, but the Rules for selling puts also follow the same basic ideas as those for calls.

The entire discussion about exercising puts versus selling them is identical to the discussion with regard to selling and exercising calls in Chapter 5. In short, it always makes more sense to sell the put option than to exercise it. The reason for this is that if the price of a particular series of puts declined so far that it was more profitable to exercise it, the floor traders, who do not pay commissions, would immediately take advantage of such an opportunity. They would be buying the puts, exercising them, and immediately buying the underlying stock in the market to cover the short position. Their activity would bid the price of the puts up to the level where the entire operation would cease to be profitable.

Rule 5: SELLING THE OPTIONS YOU OWN IS ALWAYS BETTER THAN EXERCISING THEM AND THEN CLOSING THE RESULTING POSITION IN THE UNDERLYING STOCK.

Your targets for the underlying stock are as important when you are dealing in puts as when you are dealing in calls. Once reached, they automatically trigger profit-taking:

Rule 6: SELL THE OPTIONS YOU OWN AS SOON AS THE UNDERLYING STOCK HAS REACHED YOUR TARGET.

At the beginning of this chapter, we discussed the Rule that requires a stricter discipline from the put owner than from the call owner. Since the downside for the underlying stock is limited, the put owner should not move his original target down in an attempt to squeeze a few more points out of his puts:

Rule 17: A PUT OWNER SHOULD NEVER MOVE DOWN HIS ORIGINAL TARGET FOR THE UNDERLYING STOCK. THE PROFIT SHOULD BE TAKEN AS SOON AS THE ORIGINAL TARGET IS REACHED.

The similarity continues in the situations when the forecast of the underlying stock has changed for the worse. Both the put owner and the call owner should sell their respective positions if and when they can salvage 50% of the initial investment. Failing that, they should sell the options on the expiration day if there are buyers.

Rule 7: DO NOT SELL THE OPTIONS YOU OWN AT A LOSS EARLIER THAN ON THE EXPIRATION DAY, UNLESS YOUR FORECAST OF THE UNDERLYING STOCK HAS CHANGED.

Rule 8: IF YOU BOUGHT OPTIONS AND THEN YOUR FORECAST OF THE UNDERLYING STOCK HAS CHANGED FOR THE WORSE, SELL THE OPTIONS ONLY WHEN YOU CAN GET 50% OR MORE OF THE PURCHASE PRICE BACK (AFTER COMMISSIONS). IF YOU CANNOT DO THAT, SELL THE OPTIONS ON THE EXPIRATION DAY.

The strategies of buying calls and buying puts are so similar from the analytical point of view that most books on options treat them one after the other. However, I prefer treating them separately, even in different chapters. The reason is that the two strategies represent completely different expectations of the behaviour of the underlying stock. Buying calls is bullish, while buying puts is bearish. In my view, being bullish or bearish on the stock is the most important decision in the chain of the investment steps leading to profits.

2. Writing Calls

The analogy with Chapter 5 does not end as we switch from buying puts to writing calls. In that chapter we discussed the situation in which you were bullish on the underlying stock, but could find no calls that would satisfy all the pertinent Rules. My recommendation was to investigate the possibility of writing puts.

Similarly, when you are bearish on the underlying stock, you might not find any puts that you could buy without violating any of the Rules set out in this chapter. Under such circumstances, you should look into writing calls.

Let us consider an example. On October 10, 1980, ASA was trading at $91.00 US on the New York Stock Exchange. Imagine that you were bearish on ASA and expected it to decline to $75.00 US before the end of January, 1981. You considered buying puts as the most natural first step in your strategic approach to the situation. Rule 2 suggested that February puts were the best choice as far as the expiration month was concerned.

A call to your broker revealed the following:

> February 50 puts were trading at $0.31 US,
> February 60 puts were trading at $0.69 US,
> February 70 puts were trading at $2.00 US,
> February 80 puts were trading at $4.50 US,
> February 90 puts were trading at $9.00 US,

None of the above puts would comply with Rule 4. A quick calculation will verify that when ASA reached your target of $75.00 US, the above listed puts would have the following intrinsic values:

February 50 puts: $0.00 US,
February 60 puts: $0.00 US,
February 70 puts: $0.00 US,
February 80 puts: $5.00 US,
February 90 puts: $15.00 US,

Even though February 80 and 90 puts would make a profit, they would not double the initial investment and, therefore, had to be rejected under Rule 4.

So you could not buy puts without breaking the Rules. And you certainly were not going to break those Rules because your goal was to increase the chances for making a profit.

The next logical step was to investigate the possibility of writing calls. Rule 10 recommended that you stayed with the same expiration month:

Rule 10: WRITE ONLY THOSE OPTIONS WHICH HAVE BETWEEN 2 AND 5 MONTHS UNTIL EXPIRATION.

The rationale here is exactly the same as in the case of puts. The closer to expiration, the lower the option prices, be it calls or puts. Writing very cheap calls does not make much sense because the price you receive for them will not be worth the trouble. Writing the calls with very long life is dangerous because you leave the underlying stock too much time to move against you. As with puts, the best course of action is a happy medium.

According to Rule 10, if you were going to write any calls, it would have to be February calls. Another call to the broker brought the following information:

February 50 calls were trading at $41.25 US,
February 60 calls were trading at $32.75 US,
February 70 calls were trading at $24.25 US,
February 80 calls were trading at $17.88 US,
February 90 calls were trading at $12.50 US.

Should you write any of them and if yes, then which one? In order to answer this question we must turn to Rule 9:

Rule 9: WRITE ONLY OUT-OF-THE-MONEY OPTIONS WHICH ARE THE CLOSEST TO BEING AT-THE-MONEY.

The rationale behind this Rule is that when you write an option, be it a call or a put, with the intention of buying it back later, you do not want it to be exercised. Remember, when the option is exercised, you pay the commission on buying or selling the underlying stock. When you close the stock position, you pay another commission. Both commissions bite right into your profit.

Options are exercised only when they are in-the-money, i.e. when they have a positive intrinsic value. That is why you want to write only out-of-the-money options, whether calls or puts. On the other hand, you would like to receive as much for the option you are writing as possible. For that reason you want to write the options that are close to being at-the-money, since far out-of-the-money options are too cheap.

Applying Rule 9 to ASA February calls, you find that none of them is suitable for writing, since all of them are in-the-money and can be expected to be exercised at any time.

Let us assume, however, that you waited for a few days and saw ASA decline to $88.00 US and February 90 calls to $10.00 US. Now February 90 calls have become acceptable under Rules 9 and 10.

It is time to build the Profit/Loss Profile of a call writer.

What if ASA continued to decline and reached, say, $85.00 US? Since you are short a call, you have no control over its exercise. All the cards are in the hands of the buyer, as we have already discussed (see Chapter 5):

ALL THE STRATEGIES RELATED TO WRITING OPTIONS MUST BE ANALYZED FIRST FROM THE STANDPOINT OF THE BUYER, SINCE IT IS THE BUYER WHO DETERMINES IF THE OPTION WILL BE EXERCISED.

When ASA declined to $85.00 US, the intrinsic value of February 90 calls would become zero. Consequently, the owner of the calls would not exercise them. The calls would expire worthless and you, the writer of the calls, would have kept the $10.00 US received for them.

Exactly the same thing would happen at any price of ASA below $90.00 US.

What if ASA rallied to $105.00 US? At this price, the intrinsic value of February 90 calls would soar to $15.00 US. It would make sense for the owner of the calls to exercise them. By exercising the calls, he would buy the stock from you at $90.00 US. Since you did not own ASA in the first place, selling the stock to the call owner would make you short ASA at a price of $90.00 US. Since you are not interested in maintaining the short position, you would immediately close it by buying the stock back in the market at $105.00 US.

As a result of all these transactions, you would sustain a loss of $105.00 − $90.00 = $15.00 US on the stock alone. This loss would be reduced by the $10.00 US received for the calls at the time of writing. Your resulting net loss would amount to $15.00 − $10.00 = $5.00 US per share.

Repeating similar calculations for various prices of ASA, we can fill in the table as in Figure 7. The same information can be presented in graph form as in Figure 8:

Stock Price	Profit or Loss
$ 1.00	$ +10.00
50.00	+10.00
80.00	+10.00
90.00	+10.00
91.00	+9.00
92.00	+8.00
93.00	+7.00
94.00	+6.00
95.00	+5.00
96.00	+4.00
97.00	+3.00
98.00	+2.00
99.00	+1.00
100.00	0.00
101.00	−1.00
105.00	−5.00
110.00	−10.00
150.00	−50.00
200.00	−100.00

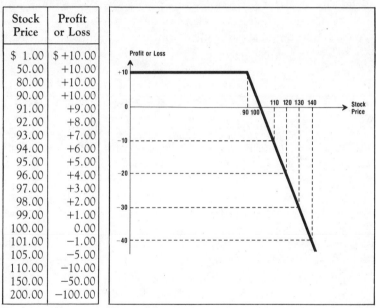

Figure 7   **Figure 8**

As you can see, the profit of the call writer is limited by the amount of money received for the calls. The potential risk, on the other hand is unlimited. The higher the underlying stock goes, the greater the loss. The Profit/Loss Potential of a call writer is very similar to that of a put writer. There are only two differences. First, the call writer makes a profit when the underlying stock declines, while the put writer profits from rallies. Second, the potential loss of a put writer is large but limited (see Figure 4), while the potential loss of a call writer is unlimited. Consequently, writing calls requires even more caution than writing puts.

What is the worst possible scenario for a call writer? Obviously, the greatest harm would be done by a rally so sharp that the Exchange halts trading in the underlying stock. When that happens, call and put options on the stock also stop trading. The stock eventually re-opens for trading at a new level which can be much higher than that at the time of the trading halt. When the stock and its options are not trading, one cannot close a position until trading re-opens. The higher re-opening price of the underlying stock, the larger the loss of a call writer.

Even though it is impossible to foresee all possible causes of unexpected sharp rallies, such as oil or gold finds or repurchasing of shares by the issuing corporation, the single most common source of sudden jumps can be determined in advance. At least 90% of all sudden rallies in individual stocks result from take-overs or take-over rumours. In order to avoid being caught in one of those, you should follow this simple Rule:

Rule 18: BEFORE WRITING UNCOVERED CALLS, MAKE SURE THAT THE UNDERLYING STOCK IS NOT A POTENTIAL TAKE-OVER CANDIDATE.

What does it mean practically? Simply call your broker and ask him or her. Make sure that your broker understands that you are not interested in just the rumours about a possible take-over. Of course, if there has been such a rumour with regard to the underlying stock, the last thing you want to do is to write uncovered calls against it. But you are also interested in such take-over attractions as a large amount of cash on the corporate balance sheet or a massive tax loss which could be used by a potential buyer.

One good way to eliminate the take-over risk is to write uncovered calls only on the stocks that are too big for a take-over, such as IBM., General Motors, Bell Canada, etc.

Once you have taken all possible precautions against walking into a take-over disaster, it is time to concentrate on the Reward/Risk Ratio. Remember, whatever strategies and investment vehicles you are using, the main goal is to keep your total profit larger than your total loss. The best way to do it is to be right more often than wrong (which depends on good stock forecasting) and to make more when you are right than you lose when you are wrong. In other words, you have to keep the Reward/Risk Ratio above 100%.

The Profit/Loss Profile of a call writer, presented on Figures 7 and 8, suggests that it is not as easy as it is for an option buyer. The potential profit of a call writer is severely limited, while the potential loss has no limit. As in the case of writing puts, the technique of mental stop-loss comes to the rescue:

Rule 19: WHEN WRITING CALLS, PLACE A MENTAL STOP-LOSS AT THE PRICE WHICH IS EQUAL TO THE PRICE OF THE UNDERLYING STOCK AT THE TIME OF WRITING PLUS THE PRICE OF THE CALL.

In other words, when the underlying stock moves up (which means against you) exactly as far as the price you received for the calls, you should admit the defeat and buy the calls back at the market price. Since calls usually grow more slowly in dollar terms then the underlying stock, your loss will be smaller than the total price received for the calls.

Returning to the example of ASA: if you wrote February 90 calls for $10.00 US when the stock was trading at $88.00 US, the proper level for mental stop-loss would be $88.00 + $10.00 = $98.00 US. If ASA indeed moved from $88.00 US to $98.00 US, it is very improbable that the calls would run up from $10.00 US to $20.00 US. Even if the rally in the stock was swift, the calls would most probably reach $15.00 - $16.00 US. By buying them back at this level, you would have incurred a loss much smaller than the full price of $10.00 US received for the calls. This would help your Reward/Risk Ratio to remain above 100% in the long run.

An experienced trader could stop me at this point with the following comment: Using Rule 19 in situations where the price of options written is relatively low would result in being "stopped out" after an insignificant move in the underlying stock. This comment, which I have heard many times during my career as an option strategist, is certainly valid. If you write cheap options, the use of a stop-loss becomes self-defeating. The catch is in the fact that you should *never* write cheap options!

Indeed, the maximum profit you can make by writing a call or put option is the price received for it. Therefore, you should not write any option whose price is too low. You must always remember that from time to time even the mental stop-loss will fail to save you from being caught in a large move in the wrong direction. Once in a while you will encounter a relatively large loss. Therefore, when you are making a profit, it should not be so small that you need an electronic microscope to see it!

Rule 11: WRITE ONLY THOSE OPTIONS WHOSE PRICE IS AT LEAST 10% OF THE STRIKE PRICE.

This Rule will prevent you from falling into a popular trap of writing far out-of-the-money calls (Rule 9 would have the same effect). In fact, this trap is so popular that many advisers recommend it as a winning strategy! These advisers rationalize that the prices of far out-of-the-money call options represent unreasonable expectations of wild gamblers. If someone is crazy enough to buy a call option with the strike price of $40 when the underlying stock is trading at $30, they say, let us write such an option and benefit from his craziness. The stock will obviously never get to $40 and we will keep the money received.

The error in this argument is hidden in the word "never." The correct statement is that *most of the time* the underlying stock fails to stage a spectacular rally and far out-of-the-money calls expire worthless. The buyers of these calls are not as crazy as those advisers think. When buying far out-of-the-money calls, the gamblers pay very low prices, like 5¢ - 10¢ per share. Those who write far out-of-the-money calls across the board make scores of small profits as the calls expire worthless. Once in a while, however, they get caught in a take-over or another unexpected event which sends the underlying stock through the stratosphere. A huge loss wipes out dozens of microscopic profits. Over a long period of time the followers of this strategy end up losing quite a lot of money paid as brokerage commissions.

This is but one more illustration to the general rule that there is no easy way to make big money in options or in any other field. THERE IS NO FREE LUNCH! One has to work to earn a profit. In the case of options, one must analyze the underlying stock and then follow all the Rules in chapter 2 in order to get ahead and stay ahead.

We have covered all the Rules which help you to select the best calls for writing. As soon as you know which calls you are going to write, the question arises: how many of them you can afford to write? Rule 16 provides the answer that is universal for calls and puts:

Rule 16: WHEN WRITING UNCOVERED OPTIONS, THE AMOUNT OF MONEY YOU RECEIVE SHOULD NOT EXCEED THE AMOUNT OF MONEY YOU ARE PREPARED TO LOSE.

We have examined this Rule in detail in chapter 5. In short, your mental stop-loss, as defined by Rule 19, will limit most of your losses to an amount smaller than your total receipts from the sale of calls. Therefore, the amount of money you receive when writing options becomes a measure of risk.

The Rules for closing short positions in call options are identical to those for closing short positions in put options. These Rules have also been analyzed in chapter 5 and we do not have to dwell on them here.

First, don't try to squeeze the last penny out of your short positions:

Rule 13: COVER YOUR SHORT POSITIONS AS SOON AS YOU CAN MAKE A PROFIT (AFTER COMMISSIONS) EQUAL TO 75% OF THE INITIAL PRICE OF THE OPTION.

Second, be prepared to abandon any position that has turned sour. You could sit and wait when you were a buyer of options, but being a writer, you should run for your life as soon as the first drops of rain wet the pavement. Remember, the losses could be horrendous!

Rule 14: IF YOUR FORECAST OF THE UNDERLYING STOCK HAS CHANGED UNFAVOURABLY, CLOSE ALL SHORT POSITIONS IMMEDIATELY.

Third, do not change your strategy in the middle of the game. When you are applying all the Rules to select the best call option to write, your intentions are to write the option and to buy it back later at a lower price. You are not planning to have the calls exercised and to maintain the resulting short position in the underlying stock. Therefore, if the calls are indeed exercised, you should not alter the game plan:

Rule 15: IF YOU WROTE OPTIONS WITH THE INTENTION OF BUYING THEM BACK LATER, AND THEY WERE EXERCISED, IMMEDIATELY CLOSE THE RESULTING STOCK POSITION.

As was illustrated in chapter 5, having your short options exercised can often be a blessing if you close the stock position right away. First, since you would only write out-of-the-money options, they would be exercised only when the underlying stock has moved against your forecast. In such circumstances, buying the option back would result in a loss, while having it exercised might still leave you with a profit. Since you are not buying the exercised option back, you get to keep the entire amount of money received for it at the time of writing. This amount will often prove sufficient to cover a small loss on the stock together with commissions.

Of course, this does not mean that you should sit and wait for your short options to be exercised, ignoring the mental stop-loss. Rule 15 applies only to those situations where your short options are exercised *before* the mental stop-loss has been reached.

Now you know all the Rules you should follow in those cases

when you are bearish on the underlying stock. The Rules are designed in such a way as to eliminate unreasonably risky situations and to highlight the most profitable ones.

Quite often you will find that these Rules will eliminate all available puts as inappropriate for buying and all available calls as inappropriate for writing. What should you do then, if you are bearish on the underlying stock?

My advice is to forget about options. If your conviction is strong enough, sell the stock short. Above all, do not bend the Rules!

Options, like any other investment vehicle, can make you money as long as you don't fall in love with them. Yet it is not very easy, especially after a few highly profitable trades. I hope that my Rules will help you to keep your head cool. Remember, in the long run, only cool heads stay above water!

Chapter 7

Recommended Strategies — Neutral
1. Buying Straddles
2. Buying Combinations
3. Writing Straddles
4. Writing Combinations

1. Buying Straddles

In this chapter we are going to analyze four strategies that I call "neutral." In my terminology, a "neutral" strategy is one that is neither bullish nor bearish. This might be confusing for an investor who is used to buying and selling stocks exclusively. If such an investor is neither bullish nor bearish on a stock, it simply means that he has no opinion on the stock whatsoever. If he knows nothing about the stock, how can options possibly make money for him?

The correct answer is, of course, negative. Nothing will help you to make a profit on the stock if you cannot forecast its behaviour. This fact, which is a direct corollary of the Basic Law of Nature, the law which states that THERE IS NO FREE LUNCH, was the subject of my first Confession:

Confession 1: IN ORDER TO MAKE MONEY IN OPTIONS, YOU MUST HAVE A REASONABLE FORECAST OF THE BEHAVIOUR OF THE UNDERLYING STOCK.

In view of this Confession, how can a "neutral" strategy work? The answer lies in the fact that the range of possible behaviour of stock prices is much wider than simply going up or down. To illustrate this point, let us assume that you could know for sure that a particular stock would be trading six months from now at the current price. Would that information be sufficient for describing the behaviour of the stock during the entire six month period? Obviously not. The stock could conceivably move up and then return to the original level. Or it could decline and then move back up. It could also do absolutely nothing or fluctuate around the initial price.

It is obvious that the more you know about the behaviour of a stock, the more opportunities you have to use this information for making a profit. For example, if you knew that the stock you were interested in was going to participate in a strong rally and then fall back to the original price, you could certainly profit from this information by buying the stock immediately and selling it during the rally. On the other hand, if you knew that the stock was going to move less than 2% during the entire 6 month period, you could not make money by either buying it or selling it short. Another situation in which you could not turn your information into a profit by either buying or shorting the stock is if you expected it to move sharply but could not predict the direction of the move.

This is where "neutral" option strategies help. To see how they work, let us start with an example. On June 12, 1984, Bow Valley Industries was trading at $25.00 Cdn. On the same day Bow Valley January 25 calls were trading at $2.50 Cdn. and January 25 puts were trading at $1.50 Cdn. Imagine that you bought both a January 25 call and a January 25 put.

At first it doesn't seem to make much sense. You buy calls when you are bullish on the underlying stock and you buy puts when you are bearish. Why should you buy both calls and puts at the same time? Is it possible to be both bullish and bearish on the same stock at the same time?

In order to find answers to these questions, let us examine the Profit/Loss Profile of the resulting position. When you bought the call and the put with the same strike price and the same expiration month, in the jargon of options you bought *a straddle*. In our example, you bought a Bow Valley Industries January 25 straddle. Since you paid $2.50 Cdn. for the call and $1.50 Cdn. for the put, your total cost was $2.50 + $1.50 = $4.00 Cdn. per share.

If Bow Valley Industries stayed at exactly $25.00 Cdn. until the expiry in January, both January 25 calls and January 25 puts would expire worthless. In that case you would have lost your entire investment of $4.00 Cdn. per share.

If Bow Valley Industries moved up to $35.00 Cdn., your January 25 put would become totally useless, while the January 25 call would acquire an intrinsic value of $10.00 Cdn. By selling the call alone you could make a profit of $10.00 − $4.00 = $6.00 Cdn.

If instead of staging a spectacular rally to $35.00 Cdn., Bow Valley declined to $15.00 Cdn., your January 25 call would have no value. The January 25 put, however, would become quite valuable. Its intrinsic value would reach $10.00 Cdn. By selling the put alone, you could make a profit of $10.00 − $4.00 = $6.00 Cdn.

Repeating similar calculations for different prices of Bow Valley

Industries, we can fill in the table as in Figure 9. The same information can be presented in the form of a graph as in Figure 10:

Stock Price	Profit or Loss
$ 1.00	$ +20.00
10.00	+11.00
15.00	+6.00
20.00	+1.00
21.00	0.00
22.00	−1.00
23.00	−2.00
24.00	−3.00
25.00	−4.00
26.00	−3.00
27.00	−2.00
28.00	−1.00
29.00	0.00
30.00	+1.00
35.00	+6.00
40.00	+11.00
50.00	+21.00
100.00	+71.00

Figure 9

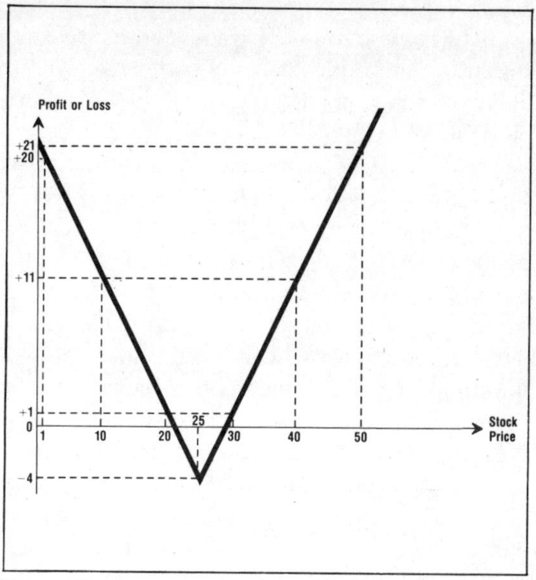

Figure 10

Figures 9 and 10 show that the owner of a straddle makes a profit either when the underlying stock moves far up or when it drops far down. The move should be so large that the profit made by one option covers the cost of both the call and the put. Small moves in either direction leave the straddle owner with a loss, and the smaller the move, the larger the loss.

Such a Profit/Loss Profile suggests that straddles should be purchased only in special situations. One such situation arises when a company is involved in a major lawsuit. If the size of the lawsuit is such that an upset in court could endanger the financial health of the corporation, the price of its stock will be depressed to a certain extent several months before the hearing. If the lawsuit is lost, the stock would plummet further. If the corporation wins the case, however, the stock will immediately rally from its depressed level. Under these conditions, it is wise to buy a straddle a few weeks before the hearing. The greatest risk in taking such a position lies in the possibility of the hearing being postponed. You must always remember that an option owner cannot wait forever:

Rule 2: YOU SHOULD ONLY BUY THOSE OPTIONS WHICH WILL EXPIRE AFTER THE TIME PERIOD DURING WHICH YOU EXPECT THE UNDERLYING STOCK TO REACH YOUR TARGET.

Another situation that happens frequently, which suggests the possibility of buying a straddle, is related to exploration companies. For example, if an oil company is involved in a major drilling project, it might be wise to buy a straddle on its stock a few weeks before the results are announced. If the company strikes oil, the stock is very likely to stage a strong rally, but if the hole is dry, the stock will most probably sell off.

In fact, any pending announcement, which might have a major impact, is a signal for considering a straddle.

There are other possible situations when buying a straddle might make sense, and all such situations have one thing in common. You must have a good reason to expect a strong move in the underlying stock, but you might not be able to forecast the direction of the move. This is precisely why I call buying straddles "a neutral strategy." The information which suggests that buying a straddle is a reasonable investment decision can be classified neither as bullish nor as bearish. Nevertheless, it is valid and important information that is sufficient for making a profitable investment.

This is the principle difference between buying straddles and the strategies analyzed in the previous chapter. Buying calls and writing puts are bullish strategies. As such, they are supplementary to buying the underlying stock. Indeed, if you are bullish on the stock, you can simply buy it. There must be an additional benefit in using one of the bullish option strategies, instead of buying the stock itself. The same applies to buying puts and writing calls. These strategies are supplementary to selling the underlying stock short.

Buying straddles is not a supplementary strategy. Even if you knew with absolute certainty that on a given day a major lawsuit against a company was going to be settled, and if you also knew that the settlement would create a 25% move, but you could not predict the direction of the move, there would be no way for you to benefit from all that knowledge without the use of options. You couldn't be sure of making a profit by either buying the stock or selling it short. Options provide a vehicle for making profits in such "neutral" situations.

Let us now return to the Profit/Loss Profile of a straddle owner. What is his maximum possible loss? Figures 9 and 10 indicate that the maximum loss is limited by the amount of money paid for the straddle. Therefore, Rule 1 applies to straddles as well as to calls and puts: .

Rule 1: NEVER PUT MORE MONEY INTO BUYING OPTIONS THAN YOU ARE PREPARED TO LOSE.

If you compare the Profit/Loss Profile of a straddle buyer with that of a call buyer, you will notice an interesting detail. Even though both have a chance to lose the entire investment, the probability of that happening to the call buyer is much higher than to a straddle buyer. Indeed, if the underlying stock moves down and stays below the strike price, the owner of the call will lose his total investment. It doesn't really matter how far down the stock goes as long as it stays below the strike price.

The position of a straddle buyer is much better. In order for him to lose all the money invested in the straddle, the underlying stock must be trading exactly at the strike price on the day of expiration. At any other price, the straddle owner will get some of his money back or may even make a profit! Therefore, it is very rare that a straddle buyer will lose his entire investment. This fact allows the buyers of straddles to settle for smaller profits than those required for call buyers in order to create the Reward/Risk Ratio greater than 100%:

Rule 21: YOU SHOULD BUY ONLY THOSE STRADDLES WHICH WILL MAKE A 50% PROFIT (AFTER COMMISSIONS) WHEN THE UNDERLYING STOCK REACHES ONE OF YOUR TARGETS.

Rule 21 suggests that you *must* have definite targets in mind when buying a straddle. As in the case of buying calls and puts, it is the need to keep the Reward/Risk Ratio above 100% that requires definite targets. What is different from buying calls or puts, is that when buying a straddle you need two targets: one on the upside and one on the downside. The reason is that if the underlying stock rallies, the call you bought must become expensive enough to pay for the price of the entire straddle plus to generate sufficient profit. If the underlying stock plummets, it is up to the put to pay for the straddle and to bring a gain on top of it. In order to check if the expected move in either direction would achieve these goals, you must have specific targets on either side.

It is obvious that the less you pay for a straddle, the smaller move it will take to satisfy Rule 21 and the higher the probability of such a move happening during the lifetime of the straddle. The following Rule is very helpful in selecting the cheapest straddles possible.

Rule 20: YOU SHOULD BUY STRADDLES ONLY WHEN THE PRICE OF THE UNDERLYING STOCK IS WITHIN ONE DOLLAR OF THE STRIKE PRICE.

Once you own a straddle, you have nothing better to do than to sit and wait for the underlying stock to make the expected move. As soon as it happens, you must take profits by selling the option which is in-the-money. In other words, if the underlying stock has rallied to your upper target, you should sell the call, because it is the call that has generated a profit. If the stock has declined to your lower target, you should obviously sell the put.

Why shouldn't you sell both sides of the straddle? The reason is quite simple. After a strong rally your puts will be worth very little. The same will apply to the calls after a substantial decline in the stock price. You will not make much additional money by selling those options that have lost most of their value. On the other hand, if you keep them, there is always a chance of the stock returning close to its initial price, at which time you would be able to sell the remaining option at a much better price.

Rule 22: IF YOU OWN A STRADDLE OR A COMBINATION AND THE UNDERLYING STOCK HAS REACHED ONE OF YOUR TARGETS, YOU MUST SELL THE OPTION WHICH IS MAKING A PROFIT AND KEEP THE OTHER OPTION.

In order to illustrate this Rule, let us return to the example of Bow Valley Industries. If you remember, on June 12, 1984, you bought a January 25 call at $2.50 Cdn. and a January 25 put at $1.50 Cdn. In other words, you bought a January 25 straddle at $2.50 + $1.50 = $4.00 Cdn. per share. At that time, the underlying stock was trading at $25.00 Cdn. Let us also assume that your targets for the stock were $30.00 Cdn. on the upside and $20.00 Cdn. on the downside.

In the following few weeks Bow Valley Industries went into a tailspin and on July 13, 1984, it reached the target of $20.00 Cdn. According to Rule 22, this was the time to sell your January 25 put. The put was trading at $5.00 Cdn. and by selling it you could make a profit of $5.00 − $4.00 = $1.00 Cdn. You could also sell your January 25 call for $0.50 Cdn., but Rule 22 would suggest that you keep it. If you followed this Rule, you would be rewarded for the patience. By September 4, 1984, Bow Valley Industries had returned to the $25.00 Cdn. level, which created the opportunity to sell January 25 calls for $1.25 Cdn.! This sale would increase your profit on the straddle to $1.00 + $1.25 = $2.25 Cdn. This is an excellent example of having your cake and eating it too!

The above example illustrated the best thing that can happen to a straddle buyer: first the stock moves one way; reaches the target; you sell one of the options for a profit; then the stock returns to the original level and you sell the other option.

The worst scenario is when the underlying stock keeps fluctuating around its initial price without making a major move. As time goes, the prices of both your call and your put begin to decline and you are tempted to sell them both at a loss and to forget about the whole thing. Resist the temptation! Remember that you bought the straddle in expectation of a particular event which was supposed to produce a strong influence on the price of the underlying stock. That event might happen even a few days before expiration and still produce the expected profit for you. In this situation, patience is a virtue and it should be practised as prescribed by Rules 7 and 8:

Rule 7: DO NOT SELL THE OPTIONS YOU OWN AT A LOSS EARLIER THAN ON THE EXPIRATION DAY, UNLESS YOUR FORECAST OF THE UNDERLYING STOCK HAS CHANGED.

Rule 8: IF YOU BOUGHT OPTIONS AND THEN YOUR FORECAST OF THE UNDERLYING STOCK CHANGED FOR THE WORSE, SELL THE OPTIONS ONLY WHEN YOU CAN GET 50% OR MORE OF THE PURCHASE PRICE BACK (AFTER COMMISSIONS). IF YOU CANNOT DO THAT, SELL THE OPTIONS ON THE EXPIRATION DAY.

Buying straddles is the first of the four neutral strategies examined in this chapter. The other three are very similar to this one, so if you get a good handle on buying straddles, you will find it easy to deal with the rest of the material in this chapter.

2. Buying Combinations

From time to time you will face situations where buying a straddle would seem like the right strategy and all the required conditions will be met except for Rule 20. In other words, you will be expecting a major move in the underlying stock within a specified period of time. Both calls and puts will seem to be cheap relative to the size of the expected move. The direction of the move would be uncertain and, therefore, you would be ready to buy a straddle. The only stumbling block will be the fact that the price of the underlying stock is not close enough to any of the strike prices.

For example, let us assume that you expected a large move one way or the other in Coca-Cola, when the stock was trading at $62.50 US. The closest strike prices were $60.00 US and $65.00 US Since Coca-Cola was $2.50 US away from either of the strike prices, Rule 20 prohibited buying a straddle.

Was there anything you could do to capitalize on your expectations of a large move? Fortunately, the answer is yes. The proper course of action was to buy a February 65 call (which was trading at $2.75 US) and a February 60 put (which was trading at $1.75 US). Even though the call and the put both had the same expiration month of February, their respective strike prices were different. Consequently, the position you acquired was not a straddle. Such positions are called "combinations." The name is not so widespread as to become universal, and I have heard this position called all kinds of things, including a poetic name such as "wings."

As we have been doing so far, in order to get better acquainted with a new options position, we will build its Profit/Loss Profile.

If Coca-Cola moved up just a little bit and reached $64.00 US by the expiration time, both January 65 calls and January 60 puts would expire worthless. As a result, you would have lost your entire investment of $2.75 + $1.75 = $4.50 US. In fact, the situation would be exactly the same at any price of Coca-Cola between $60.00 US and $65.00 US.

If the stock rallied to $75.00 US, your February 65 call would acquire the intrinsic value of $10.00 US, while the February 60 put would become worthless. By selling the call alone at its intrinsic value, you would make a profit of $10.00 − $4.50 = $5.50 US.

If instead of rallying to $75.00 US, Coca-Coal declined to $50.00 US, the February 65 call would lose its entire value, while the February 60 put would become worth at least $10.00 US. Again, your profit would amount to $10.00 − $4.50 = $5.50 US.

Repeating similar calculations for various prices of Coca-Cola, we can easily fill in the table as in Figure 11. The same information can be presented in graph form as in Figure 12.

As you can see, the Profit/Loss Profile of a combination is very similar to that of a straddle. Consequently, most of the Rules applicable to buying straddles are also applicable to buying combinations.

First of all, like any option position, a combination has only a limited lifespan. Since time is never on the side of an option buyer (which means that if nothing happens with the underlying stock until expiration, you will most probably lose most or all of your money), you must be very careful in selecting the expiration month of the combination:

Rule 2: YOU SHOULD BUY ONLY THOSE OPTIONS WHICH WILL EXPIRE AFTER THE TIME PERIOD DURING WHICH YOU EXPECT THE UNDERLYING STOCK TO REACH YOUR TARGET.

Second, the Profit/Loss Profile clearly indicates that a combina-

Stock Price	Profit or Loss
$ 1.00	$ +54.50
20.00	+35.50
40.00	+15.50
55.00	+0.50
55.50	0.00
56.00	−0.50
58.00	−2.50
59.00	−3.50
60.00	−4.50
61.00	−4.50
64.00	−4.50
65.00	−4.50
66.00	−3.50
67.00	−2.50
69.00	−0.50
69.50	0.00
70.00	+0.50
80.00	+10.50
100.00	+30.50
200.00	+130.50

Figure 11   Figure 12

tion buyer can lose his entire investment. Therefore, Rule 1 must be consulted before entering into the position:

Rule 1: NEVER PUT MORE MONEY INTO BUYING OPTIONS THAN YOU ARE PREPARED TO LOSE.

The next task is to ascertain that the Reward/Risk Ratio related to buying combinations is above 100% on the average. This is one area where combinations differ materially from straddles. Take another look at Profit/Loss Profiles of both straddles and combinations. Ask yourself, in each case, what are the chances for a total loss? Your answers will be different depending on which position you are studying, a straddle or a combination.

In the case of a straddle, the underlying stock would have to trade exactly at the strike price of the straddle on the expiration day in order for you to suffer a total loss. As we have discussed earlier in this chapter, it is not very probable. On the other hand, the owner of a straddle loses his entire investment when the underlying stock trades between the two strike prices on the expiration day. Using our earlier example of Coca-Cola, if the stock traded between $60.00 US and $65.00 US at expiration, both January 65 calls and January 60 puts would expire worthless. This would result in a total loss by the straddle owner.

Since the owner of a combination has a higher probability of losing his entire investment than a straddle owner, the potential profits on a combination must also be higher than those on a straddle. Consequently, instead of Rule 21, which is applicable to straddles only, the buyer of a combination must follow Rule 4:

Rule 4: YOU SHOULD BUY ONLY THOSE OPTIONS WHICH WILL DOUBLE THEIR PURCHASE PRICE (AFTER COMMISSIONS) WHEN THE UNDERLYING STOCK REACHES YOUR TARGET.

Of course, you have to interpret this Rule when applying it to combinations. First of all, as in the case of straddles, you will have two targets — for a rally and for a decline. Second, when one of the targets is reached, only one of the two options will be making a profit. After a rally, the call will become the bread earner, while after a decline, this role will be assumed by the put. Rule 4 demands that whichever option produces a profit, this profit should be sufficient to double the entire investment in the combination.

Let us return to our example of Coca-Cola as in illustration. Since you were going to pay $4.50 US for the combination, Rule 4 established the minimum satisfactory profit as $2 \times \$4.50 = \$9.00$ US. In order for a January 65 call to acquire an intrinsic value of $9.00 US, Coca-Cola had to rally to $65.00 + \$9.00 = \$74.00$ US. On the downside, if the January 60 put were to become worth $9.00 US based on its intrinsic value, Coca-Cola had to sell off to $60.00 - \$9.00 = \$51.00$ US. According to Rule 4, if it was unreasonable to expect Coca-Cola either to run up to $74.00 US or to drop to $51.00 US, then buying the January 65/60 straddle was not a good idea.

Moving on from buying combinations to closing them, we continue to follow the logistics and the Rules for closing straddles.

When either of your targets is reached, only one option (either the call or the put) will be making a profit. This option is the one to be sold. The other one will be practically worthless and should be kept in case the underlying stock reverses its direction. One should never miss a chance to kill two birds with one stone!

Rule 22: IF YOU OWN A STRADDLE OR A COMBINATION AND THE UNDERLYING STOCK HAS REACHED ONE OF YOUR TARGETS, YOU MUST SELL THE OPTION WHICH IS MAKING A PROFIT AND KEEP THE OTHER OPTION.

The need for patience is as much present in buying combinations as it is in buying straddles, calls, or puts. Both Rules for "sitting and waiting" apply to combinations without any modifications:

Rule 7: DO NOT SELL THE OPTIONS YOU OWN AT A LOSS EARLIER THAN ON THE EXPIRATION DAY, UNLESS YOUR FORECAST OF THE UNDERLYING STOCK HAS CHANGED.

Rule 8: IF YOU BOUGHT OPTIONS AND THEN YOUR FORECAST OF THE UNDERLYING STOCK CHANGED FOR THE WORSE, SELL THE OPTIONS ONLY WHEN YOU CAN GET 50% OR MORE OF THE PURCHASE PRICE BACK (AFTER COMMISSIONS). IF YOU CANNOT DO THAT, SELL THE OPTIONS ON THE EXPIRATION DAY.

Buying straddles and combinations are two strategies in which the investor expects a large move in the underlying stock but cannot predict the direction of this move. In other words, the investor expects a drastic increase in the volatility of the underlying stock. In other situations, there might be good reasons to expect a sharp decline in the volatility of the stock. The following two strategies have been designed to allow investors to benefit from such situations.

3. Writing Straddles

All dramatic events, especially if they were not expected, have a great impact on human imagination. Large moves in stock prices are no exception. When a stock stages a dramatic rally, human emotions heat up. Optimists start expecting the continuation of spectacular performance, while pessimists brace themselves in expectation of a sudden reversal. If the stock under consideration is optionable, both groups have access to options. Optimists rush to buy calls and pessimists line up for puts. As a result, the prices of both calls and puts rise very sharply.

In the great majority of cases, however, both optimists and pessimists are wrong. After an unusually sharp rally, stocks have a habit of slowing down and taking a break. In other words, they trade in a more or less narrow range, which frustrates the optimists who have paid too much for their calls, and the pessimists who have paid too much for their puts.

The same happens when a stock "falls out of bed." A good example of such an occurrence was provided by Tandy Corp. which fell from $64.00 US in May, 1983, to $38.00 US in August, 1983. The stock had lost 41% of its value in 3 months! The opinions with regard to Tandy became strongly polarized. Optimists expected the stock to reverse the direction of the move and to eliminate a significant portion of the loss. Pessimists, of course, could not foresee anything but the continuation of the decline.

As it happened, Tandy continued to slide, but at a much slower rate. By October, 1983, it had bottomed below $35.00 US and started a feeble rally. Optimists took that as a signal of the expected turnaround and loaded up with calls. Their enthusiasm drove the price of July 35 calls to $7.00 US. Pessimists saw the same rally as a minor "hook" designed to fool the bulls. Consequently, they lined up to buy puts. The price of July 35 puts was pushed up to $4.00 US.

I used that situation and wrote both July 35 calls and July 35 puts. In the option jargon, I *wrote a straddle*. The position itself is called *a short straddle*. As you can see, it is the exact opposite of a long straddle. Having written this straddle, I received $7.00 + $4.00 US = $11.00 US per share. All that was left to me was to sit and wait.

What were the possibilities? To answer this question, we must analyze the Profit/Loss Profile of a short straddle.

The best thing that could happen to me was for Tandy to remain in a narrow range around $35.00 US and to trade at $35.00 US at the time of expiration. In such a case, neither the calls nor the puts would be exercised and I would keep the entire amount of $11.00 US received for the straddle. Indeed, with Tandy trading at $35.00 US, the intrinsic value of both July 35 calls and July 35 puts would be zero, which means that the owners of the calls, as well as the owners of the puts, could gain nothing by exercising their options.

I would like to remind you that being short options makes one completely helpless with regard to exercising them. Full control is in the hands of the owner of the options. Therefore:

ALL THE STRATEGIES RELATED TO WRITING OPTIONS MUST BE ANALYZED FIRST FROM THE STANDPOINT OF THE OPTION BUYER, SINCE IT IS THE BUYER WHO DETERMINES IF THE OPTION IS GOING TO BE EXERCISED.

What would happen if Tandy rallied to $40.00 US? The intrinsic value of July 35 puts would be zero and, therefore, they would not be exercised. The intrinsic value of July 35 calls, however, would become $40.00 − $35.00 = $5.00 US. This means that the owner of the calls would most probably exercise them. When the calls were exercised, I would be forced to sell Tandy to the owner of the calls for $35.00 US. Since I did not own the stock, I would find myself short it at $35.00 US. In order to close the short position, I would then have to buy Tandy in the open market at the market price of $40.00 US.

Excluding commissions, I would have lost $40.00 − $35.00 = $5.00 US on the stock alone. However, I would have kept the $11.00 US received for the straddle. My net gain would be $11.00 − $5.00 = $6.00 US.

If Tandy rallied to $50.00 US instead of $40.00 US, the same chain of events would happen, but with a less pleasant result. July 35 calls would be exercised; I would find myself short the stock and would have to buy it back in the market. My loss on the stock would be $50.00 − $35.00 = $15.00 US. It would be only partially offset by the $11.00 US received for the straddle, and my net loss would be $15.00 − $11.00 = $4.00 US.

If Tandy did not rally at all and instead declined to $30.00 US, July 35 calls would be worthless and, therefore, would not be exercised. July 35 puts, however, would acquire an intrinsic value of $35.00 − $30.00 = $5.00 US. They would be exercised by the owner and I would be forced to buy Tandy shares from the owner of the puts at $35.00 US. Since I had no intention of holding the shares, I would sell them in the open market. The best price I could get for the puts would be $30.00 US, which would bring me a loss of $35.00 − $30.00 = $5.00 US on the stock alone. Since I would be keeping the $11.00 US received for the straddle, my net gain would be $11.00 − $5.00 = $6.00 US.

As on the upside, so on the downside. If Tandy declined to $20.00 US instead of $30.00 US, the same chain of events would have brought me a loss of $15.00 US on the stock alone. Considering the fact that I would have still kept the $11.00 US, my net loss would have amounted to $15.00 − $11.00 = $4.00 US.

Repeating similar calculations for a range of prices of Tandy, we can fill in the table as in Figure 13. The same information can be presented in graph form as in Figure 14.

As you can see, writing straddles is much more dangerous than buying them. The worst that could happen to a straddle owner is the loss of the money paid for the straddle, but a straddle writer is open to unlimited risk. In fact, writing a straddle is even more dangerous than writing a call or a put. The writer of a call, as well as the writer of a put, can be hurt only if the underlying stock makes a large move in the "wrong" direction. The writer of a straddle lives in fear of a large move in *any* direction!

It must be obvious by now that a straddle writer needs protection in the form of a stop-loss. Since strong rallies and sharp declines are both dangerous to the writer, he actually needs two stop-losses, one on the upside and another on the downside.

Stock Price	Profit or Loss
$ 1.00	$ −23.00
10.00	−14.00
20.00	−4.00
23.00	−1.00
24.00	0.00
25.00	+1.00
30.00	+6.00
34.00	+10.00
35.00	+11.00
36.00	+10.00
40.00	+6.00
45.00	+1.00
46.00	0.00
47.00	−1.00
50.00	−4.00
60.00	−14.00
100.00	−54.00
200.00	−154.00

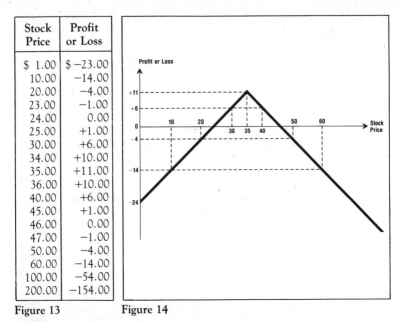

Figure 13   **Figure 14**

The exact location of the stop-losses is dictated by the necessity of maintaining a Reward/Risk Ratio of greater than 100%. As the Profit/Loss Profile on Figures 13 and 14 shows, the maximum possible gain of a straddle writer is equal to the amount of money received for the straddle. Such a gain would be realized only if the underlying stock remained close to the strike price of the straddle until expiration and if it traded exactly at the strike price at expiration. In any other case, either calls or puts would be exercised and the profit of the writer, if any, would be less than what he received for the straddle at the time of the writing.

Since the average gain of the writer, even when his forecast is correct, is smaller than the full price of the straddle, the stop-losses should be selected in such a way as to make the average loss also smaller than the price of the straddle. I recommend the following Rule:

Rule 23: WHEN WRITING A STRADDLE, PLACE ONE MENTAL STOP-LOSS AT THE PRICE EQUAL TO THE STRIKE PRICE PLUS THE TOTAL AMOUNT RECEIVED FOR THE STRADDLE, AND ANOTHER MENTAL STOP-LOSS AT THE PRICE EQUAL TO THE STRIKE PRICE MINUS THE TOTAL AMOUNT RECEIVED FOR THE STRADDLE.

In simple terms, Rule 23 recommends buying back both the call and the put, which constitute the straddle, as soon as the underlying stock moves either up or down by the amount received for the straddle.

This is a good Rule, but if it is applied to very cheap straddles, then the slightest move of the underlying stock will force the writer to close the position. Since stocks cannot be expected to remain motionless, such an application of Rule 23 would destroy the entire strategy of writing straddles. Fortunately, there is no need to modify the Rule, because *cheap straddles should not be written* under any circumstances.

Just one look at the Profit/Loss Profile will show why. The maximum possible profit of the writer is equal to the total price of the straddle. Potential losses are huge. So what is the point of writing a cheap straddle? You don't want small profits and large losses; you are aiming at the exact opposite! It follows that straddles should be written when they are very expensive:

Rule 24: WRITE ONLY THOSE STRADDLES WHOSE TOTAL PRICE IS AT LEAST 15% OF THE STRIKE PRICE.

Such high prices usually appear after a very dramatic move of the underlying stock, as happened with Tandy. The price of the July 35 straddle that I wrote was $11.00 US, which represented 31% of the strike price. My mental stop-losses, according to Rule 23, were placed at $35.00 + $11.00 = $46.00 US and at $35.00 − $11.00 = $24.00 US.

As you might have noticed, writing straddles is very similar to writing calls and puts, which really is the way it should be, since writing a straddle consists of writing a call and a put! As in writing individual options, a straddle writer is never interested in straddles that are about to expire, because they are too cheap. He is also rarely interested in straddles with very long life because the longer he has to wait, the more chances that the underlying stock will make a large move in either direction.

Rule 10: WRITE ONLY THOSE OPTIONS WHICH HAVE BETWEEN 2 AND 5 MONTHS UNTIL EXPIRATION.

When we discussed buying straddles, we came across Rule 20, which recommended buying straddles only when the underlying stock was within one dollar of the strike price. The reason was that the straddles are cheapest when the underlying stock is close to the strike price. Since the writer of a straddle does not want it to be cheap, it would seem reasonable not to write them close to the strike price. Yet the next Rule recommends doing exactly that. The reason for writing close to the strike price is, of course, entirely different from that of buying them in the same zone. Take another look at Rule 23. Note that the stop-losses are set at an equal distance from the strike price. It is obvious that when writing a straddle you would want to be as far away as possible from either of the stop-losses. The closer to them you are, the more chances of being kicked out of your position as the stock fluctuates. The farthest point from both stop-losses is right in the middle at the strike price.

Rule 25: WRITE STRADDLES ONLY WHEN THE PRICE OF THE UNDERLYING STOCK IS WITHIN ONE DOLLAR OF THE STRIKE PRICE.

Now you know everything about writing straddles — when to write them and which ones to select. It is time to talk about closing them. The analogy with writing calls and puts continues here.

The buyers of individual options and straddles need specific targets. The writers are in a better position, at least in this respect. They don't care about any targets whatsoever. The writers of calls or puts just want the underlying stock to move in the "safe" direction. The writer of a straddle hopes that the stock remains "quiet." The less the stock fluctuates, the faster the time premiums will disappear and the sooner he will be able to buy the straddle back at a price much lower than what he received for it at the time of writing.

The writer should never sit and wait until expiration in order to squeeze the last penny out of his position. As soon as he has a decent profit, he should take it and run. The next Rule defines what is "decent" or, rather, sufficient profit for a straddle writer:

Rule 26: COVER YOUR SHORT STRADDLES AND COMBINATIONS AS SOON AS YOU CAN MAKE A PROFIT (AFTER COMMISSIONS) EQUAL TO 50% OF THE TOTAL AMOUNT RECEIVED FOR THE STRADDLE OR COMBINATION.

This is exactly what happened with my straddle on Tandy. By April, 1984, the stock had slowed down, while remaining in the $30 - $40 US trading range. I bought back July 35 calls at $3.00 US and July 35 puts at $1.75 US. My profit before commissions amounted to $11.00 − $3.00 − $1.75 = $6.25 US. Even after commissions, I made slightly over 50% of the initial price of $11.00 US.

One difference between writing individual options and writing straddles is that the writer of a straddle does not mind if one of the options comprising the straddle is exercised. Imagine that you wrote a straddle and the underlying stock has moved up, but has not reached your stop-loss yet. As this point you hope that it will move back down again, because a further move up might very well trigger your mental stop-loss and leave you with a loss. If, at this point, the calls are exercised, it brings nothing but relief. Now you do not have to buy those calls back and you get to keep the time premium, which usually covers the commissions on buying and selling the underlying stock. Of course, you will have to buy back the puts, but they will be cheap. Most probably, you will end up with a profit.

The same will happen if the underlying stock declines instead of rallying, with the only difference being, that in this case the puts will be exercised.

The difference between a straddle writer and a call or put writer is that the writer of an individual option is happiest when the stock moves in the "right" direction, which excludes the possibility of the option being exercised. As far as the straddle writer is concerned, there is no "right" direction. Every move of the underlying stock endangers his position. Therefore, an exercise of one side brings relief. The most important rule is to close the position rather than change the strategy half way through the game:

Rule 27: IF ONE SIDE OF YOUR SHORT STRADDLE OR COMBINATION HAS BEEN EXERCISED, IMMEDIATELY BUY BACK THE OTHER SIDE AND CLOSE THE RESULTING STOCK POSITION.

Of course, if you are short a straddle and there is new information available about the underlying company that suggests the possibility of sharp moves, you should immediately cover your position:

Rule 14: IF YOUR FORECAST OF THE UNDERLYING STOCK HAS CHANGED UNFAVOURABLY, CLOSE ALL SHORT POSITIONS IMMEDIATELY.

One more question has to be answered every time you are prepared to write a straddle: how many contracts can you afford? The answer here is the same as that for writing calls or puts. Even though the writer receives money rather than paying it out, the total price of the straddle is the determining factor. The reason is simple. The size of the possible loss is determined by the mental stop-losses. Rule 23 links the stop-losses with the amount of money received for the straddle. As a result, this amount measures the risk of the writer.

Rule 16: WHEN WRITING UNCOVERED OPTIONS, THE AMOUNT OF MONEY YOU RECEIVE SHOULD NOT EXCEED THE AMOUNT OF MONEY YOU ARE PREPARED TO LOSE.

Unfortunately, even mental stop-losses cannot prevent an occasional large loss. We have already discussed the reasons for this in relation to writing calls and puts. The writer of a straddle writes both calls and puts at the same time; therefore, he must take all the precautions relevant to writing both kinds of options. In particular, he must follow Rule 18:

Rule 18: BEFORE WRITING UNCOVERED CALLS, MAKE SURE THAT THE UNDERLYING STOCK IS NOT A POTENTIAL TAKE-OVER CANDIDATE.

After this long list of precautions and warnings, you might ask why bother with writing straddles at all? I agree that it is not a strategy that should be used on a daily basis. However, it allows you to take advantage of situations where no other investment vehicle would generate a profit. Indeed, you would write straddles *after* a major move in the underlying stock, when it is too late to either buy the stock itself or to short it. As stock traders exchange their favourite complaint: "... if I had only known about it two weeks ago...," you would be silently writing a straddle with pretty high odds for earning a profit!

4. Writing Combinations

The difference between writing a combination and writing a straddle is exactly the same as between buying a combination and buying a straddle. You should resort to combinations in those cases when all the necessary ingredients for using a straddle are present, but the underlying stock insists on hanging between two strike prices.

For example, if you had a good reason to believe that the volatility of Moore Corp. was going to diminish sharply in the fall and winter of 1984, you could decide to write a straddle sometime in September. The problem was that the stock was trading between $50.00 Cdn. and $55.00 Cdn. and was not close enough either to $50.00 or to $55.00. Of course, you could wait until the stock came closer to one of the two strike prices, but meanwhile the option prices would have continued to decline, making the straddle less and less attractive for writing.

If you wanted to act right away, you had the opportunity to write a combination. On September 21, 1984, when Moore Corp. was trading at $52.75 Cdn., you could write a February 55 call for $2.50 Cdn. and a February 50 put for $1.20 Cdn. Having done that you would be *short a combination,* since the call and the put you wrote had the same expiry but different strike prices.

Let us examine the Profit/Loss Profile of this short combination. If Moore Corp. continued trading between $50.00 Cdn. and $55.00 Cdn. right through expiration, both February 55 calls and February 50 puts would expire worthless. In this case you would have kept the total price of the combination equal to $2.50 + $1.20 = $3.70 Cdn.

If Moore Corp. rallied up to $60.00 Cdn., your February 50 put would be worth nothing. The February 55 call, however, would have an intrinsic value of $60.00 − $55.00 = $5.00 Cdn. If the call was exercised, you would sell Moore Corp at $55.00 Cdn. Since you did not own any shares of Moore Corp. to begin with, you would be short 100 shares at $55.00 Cdn. In order to cover the short position, you would then have to buy 100 shares of Moore Corp. in the open market at the existing price of $60.00 Cdn. As a result, you would have lost $60.00 − $55.00 = $5.00 Cdn. on the stock trade alone. This loss would be reduced by the $3.70 Cdn. which you received for the combination at the time of writing. Your net loss would be equal to $5.00 − $3.70 = $1.30 Cdn.

If Moore Corp. fell down to $45.00 Cdn., instead of rallying, the February 55 call would become worthless, but the February 50 put would acquire an intrinsic value of $50.00 − $45.00 = $5.00 Cdn. If the put was exercised, you would be buying Moore Corp. at $50.00 Cdn. In order to close the stock position, you would then have to sell the stock for the market price of $45.00 Cdn. Your loss on the stock trade alone would amount to $50.00 − $45.00 = $5.00 Cdn. This loss would be reduced by the $3.70 received for the combination at the time of writing. The net loss would be equal to $5.00 − $3.70 = $1.30 Cdn.

Repeating similar calculations for various prices of Moore Corp., we could fill in the table as in Figure 15. The same information can be presented in graph form as in Figure 16.

As you can see, the Profit/Loss Profile of a short combination is quite similar to that of a short straddle. The main difference is that it is easier to keep the entire price of a combination than the entire price of a straddle. Indeed, in order for the writer of a straddle to keep the total price of the straddle, the underlying stock must trade precisely at the strike price at expiration. The probability of this happening is, obviously, quite small.

On the other hand, the writer of a combination gets to keep the total price of the combination if the underlying stock is trading

Stock Price	Profit or Loss
$ 1.00	$ −45.30
20.00	−26.30
40.00	−6.30
45.00	−1.30
46.30	0.00
47.00	+0.70
48.00	+1.70
49.00	+2.70
50.00	+3.70
51.00	+3.70
52.00	+3.70
53.00	+3.70
54.00	+3.70
55.00	+3.70
56.00	+2.70
57.00	+1.70
58.00	+0.70
58.70	0.00
59.00	−0.30
60.00	−1.30
100.00	−41.30
200.00	−141.30

Figure 15

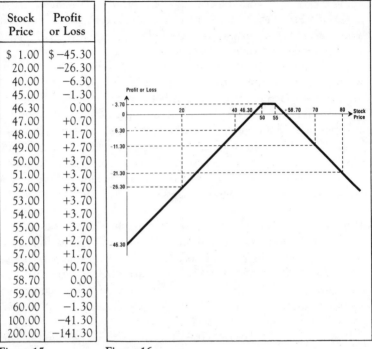

Figure 16

between the two strike prices at expiration. In our example, the writer of a combination on Moore Corp. would keep the entire price if Moore Corp. was trading between $50.00 Cdn. and $55.00 Cdn. at expiration. This is much more probable than trading at one predetermined price.

All other characteristics of short combinations are similar to those of short straddles. For example, the larger the move up or down in the underlying stock, the larger the loss of the writer.

Since it is easier to achieve the maximum possible gain when writing combinations than when writing straddles, it would seem that writing combinations is preferable to writing straddles. However, it is not true. The total amount of money received for a short straddle usually represents a higher percentage of the price of the underlying stock then the amount of money received for a short combination. The reason is very simple. When you are writing a straddle, either both the call and the put are at-the-money, or one of them is slightly out-of-the-money while the other one is in-the-money. When you are writing a combination, both options are out-of-the-money. Since at-the-money and in-the-money options are more expensive than out-of-the-money ones (other things being equal), you receive more money when writing straddles.

Consequently, one strategy is not better than the other. When you write straddles, you receive more money, but it is more difficult to keep all of it. When you write combinations, you receive less, but your chances of keeping all of it are much better.

In fact, the two strategies are not competing with each other. You should write straddles when the underlying stock is close to a strike price (see Rule 25), and you should write combinations otherwise. This way, the two strategies are complementing each other.

Due to the similarity of the Profit/Loss Profiles of short straddles and short combinations, most of the Rules applicable to short straddles are also applicable to short combinations.

To begin with, both strategies leave the investor open to potentially large losses. Therefore, stop-losses should be used:

Rule 28: WHEN WRITING A COMBINATION, PLACE ONE MENTAL STOP-LOSS AT THE PRICE EQUAL TO THE HIGHER STRIKE PRICE PLUS THE TOTAL AMOUNT RECEIVED FOR THE COMBINATION, AND ANOTHER MENTAL STOP-LOSS AT THE PRICE EQUAL TO THE LOWER STRIKE PRICE MINUS THE TOTAL AMOUNT RECEIVED FOR THE COMBINATION.

As in the case of straddles, you should never write cheap combinations. Since you can never make more than what you receive at the time of writing, you should write combinations only when they are unusually expensive, i.e. after a sharp and unexpected move in the underlying stock. However, the Rule that indicates exactly how expensive a combination should be in order for you to consider writing it, is less stringent than the corresponding Rule for straddles. Rule 24 recommended writing only those straddles that bring you at least 15% of the strike price. The following Rule, applicable to combinations, sets the lower limit at 10% of the lower strike price. The reason is that when writing a combination you have a better chance of keeping the entire proceeds than when writing a straddle.

It might help you in dealing with writing options to realize that one should always try to make about 8-10% of the price of the underlying stock when the forecast works out. When writing straddles, you must try to receive 15% or more because you will most probably get to keep only a portion of the proceeds. When writing a combination, you have a pretty good chance of keeping the total price, therefore you can settle for 10% as suggested by the following Rule:

Rule 29: WRITE ONLY THOSE COMBINATIONS WHOSE TOTAL PRICE IS AT LEAST 10% OF THE LOWER STRIKE PRICE.

Applying Rules 28 and 29 to the combination on Moore Corp., examined earlier, we would set up our mental stop-losses at $55.00 + $3.70 = $58.70 Cdn. and at $50.00 − $3.70 = $46.30 Cdn. Applying Rule 29, we would discover that the total price of the combination, which was equal to $3.70 Cdn., represented only 7% of the lower strike price, which was $50.00 Cdn. Therefore, Rule 29 would reject the Moore Corp. February 55/50 combination as too cheap for writing.

All the other Rules applicable to writing straddles apply equally to writing combinations. Since writing a combination includes writing an uncovered call, and since the greatest losses can be generated by a powerful rally in the underlying stock, you should make sure before you write a combination that you are not walking into a trap:

Rule 18: BEFORE WRITING UNCOVERED CALLS, MAKE SURE THAT THE UNDERLYING STOCK IS NOT A POTENTIAL TAKE-OVER CANDIDATE.

The usual conflict between trying to write the most expensive options and yet trying not to leave too much time for the underlying stock to move away from the strike prices, leads to the following Rule:

Rule 10: WRITE ONLY THOSE OPTIONS WHICH HAVE BETWEEN 2 AND 5 MONTHS UNTIL EXPIRATION.

You can never avoid the question of how many contracts you can afford. Even though an entire chapter of this book is devoted to cash management, some of the Rules related to cash management has already been introduced. Rule 16 applies equally to straddles and combinations:

Rule 16: WHEN WRITING UNCOVERED OPTIONS, THE AMOUNT OF MONEY YOU RECEIVE SHOULD NOT EXCEED THE AMOUNT OF MONEY YOU ARE PREPARED TO LOSE.

Closing your short positions at the right moment is as important as selecting the right positions in the first place. Closing too soon will result in gains too small to cover occasional large losses (which are, unfortunately, unavoidable). Waiting for too long would produce a high percentage of large stock moves at the last moment. Rule 26 suggests a statistically tested rule of thumb:

Rule 26: COVER YOUR SHORT STRADDLES AND
COMBINATIONS AS SOON AS YOU CAN MAKE A PROFIT
(AFTER COMMISSIONS) EQUAL TO 50% OF THE TOTAL
AMOUNT RECEIVED FOR THE STRADDLE OR COMBINATION.

When you are short a combination, as well as when you are short
a straddle, you don't really mind if one of the sides is exercised. Since
there is no "right" direction, every move of the underlying stock
brings its price closer to one of the mental stop-losses. A writer always
prefers to have one of the options exercised rather than hitting a
stop-loss. Covering your short combination at a stop-loss usually
results in a small loss, while having one of the options exercised
usually generates a small gain. Therefore, you should not be upset if
calls or puts comprising your short combination are exercised. The
most important thing, under such circumstances, is to close the
entire position immediately:

Rule 27: IF ONE SIDE OF YOUR SHORT STRADDLE OR
COMBINATION HAS BEEN EXERCISED, IMMEDIATELY BUY
BACK THE OTHER SIDE AND CLOSE THE RESULTING
STOCK POSITION.

As in the case of writing calls, puts, or straddles, being short is so
dangerous that you should run for your life at the first sign of trouble.
In other words, as soon as there is any doubt in the validity of your
original forecast due to new information, you must close your short
combination:

Rule 14: IF YOUR FORECAST OF THE UNDERLYING STOCK
HAS CHANGED UNFAVOURABLY, CLOSE ALL SHORT
POSITIONS IMMEDIATELY.

Chapter 8

Recommended Strategies — Stock Related
1. Non-Simultaneous Covered Writing
2. Buying Protective Puts
3. Replacing Stock with Calls
4. Fixing Stock Price Until Funds Are Available

1. Non-Simultaneous Covered Writing

In the previous chapters, we examined buying and writing individual options, straddles, and combinations. In every case, the investor did not own either a long or a short position in the underlying stock. In fact, wherever the options written by the investor were exercised, the best course of action was to close the resulting stock position. It was not the intention of the investor to buy, sell, or hold a position in the underlying stock.

The strategies analyzed in this chapter are fundamentally different. Instead of being an independent investment, options are treated as a supplementary tool which helps to achieve goals related to the performance of the underlying stock. The most popular of such strategies is writing calls against a long position in the underlying stock. This strategy is called "covered writing." The word "covered" indicates that the short position in the calls is protected or "covered" by the long position in the stock.

If you return to the Profit/Loss Profile of the writer of an uncovered call (Figures 7 and 8), you will recall the possibility of unlimited losses if the underlying stock skyrocketed. The reason for those huge losses was that when the short call was exercised, the writer found himself short the underlying stock at the strike price. Since he did not own the stock itself, he was forced to cover the short position by buying the stock in the market. The higher the market price of the stock, the greater the loss.

There would have been no loss at all, however, if the writer of the call had owned the underlying stock before writing the call. In that case, if and when the call was exercised, the writer would simply sell (or deliver) the stock he owned at the strike price. His profit or loss would depend on the original purchase price of the underlying stock, but not on its market price. In fact, as soon as the writer received the exercise notice, the market price would have become totally irrelevant! It is in this sense that the writer of calls who owns the underlying stock is said to be "covered."

So far we have been discussing covered writing as if it were a particular strategy. In fact, there are two fundamentally different strategies which share the same name "covered writing." These strategies are so different that one of them has found its way into this chapter among other strategies that I recommend, while the other has to wait for the next chapter, because I do not recommend it. The difference between the two strategies is in the timing of the purchase of the underlying stock.

The strategy that I recommend, and which we will examine in the following paragraphs, consists of writing calls against a long position in the underlying stock, which was purchased *before* writing calls. Some authors call this strategy "over-writing." I prefer a longer, but a more descriptive name, "non-simultaneous covered writing."

The strategy that I do not recommend consists of buying the underlying stock and writing calls against it *at the same time*. I call it "simultaneous covered writing." Another name used in the literature is "buy-writing." The reasons why I do not recommend it are explained in detail in the next chapter.

For the time being, we will concentrate on non-simultaneous covered writing. Even though this strategy involves a position in the underlying stock, the method of analysis used in the previous chapters of the book is fully applicable in this case as well. In order to analyze any option strategy, one must consider its Profit/Loss Profile.

Imagine that on October 5, 1983, you bought 100 shares of Seagram at $43.00 Cdn. Less than two months later, on November 30, 1983, the stock was trading at $49.50 Cdn. At this point you were almost ready to sell the stock. Almost — because you expected Seagram to trade above $50.00 Cdn. before it turned south. You were debating with yourself if you should sell out immediately and take a profit or wait for another dollar or two on the upside.

A friend of yours, who considered himself an experienced option player, suggested another course of action. He recommended that instead of selling the stock or waiting, you write an April 50 call on Seagram. You followed the friend's advice and received $3.00 Cdn. per share for the call. Let us examine your Profit/Loss Profile after this transaction.

First of all, as long as Seagram remains below $50.00 Cdn. the call will not be exercised. If Seagram is trading exactly at $50.00 Cdn. at expiration, you will have a $50.00 − $43.00 = $7.00 Cdn.

profit on the stock and you will also keep the $3.00 Cdn. received for the call. Your total profit will be equal to $7.00 + $3.00 = $10.00 Cdn.

If Seagram declines to $35.00 Cdn. by expiration, you will have a loss of $43.00 − $35.00 = $8.00 Cdn., which will be reduced by the $3.00 Cdn. you received for the call. The net loss would be equal to $8.00 − $3.00 = $5.00 Cdn.

If Seagram moves above $50.00 Cdn., the April 50 call would acquire an intrinsic value and could be exercised. For example, if Seagram reached $55.00 Cdn., the call could be exercised, which would force you to sell your shares for $50.00 Cdn. Your profit on the stock would amount to $50.00 − $43.00 = $7.00 Cdn. Together with the $3.00 Cdn. received for the call, it would bring your net profit to $7.00 + $3.00 = $10.00 Cdn.

Repeating similar calculations for various prices of Seagram, we could fill in the table as in Figure 17. The same information can be presented in graph form as in Figure 18:

Stock Price	Profit or Loss
$ 1.00	$ −39.00
20.00	−20.00
35.00	−5.00
39.00	−1.00
40.00	0.00
41.00	+1.00
45.00	+5.00
49.00	+9.00
50.00	+10.00
51.00	+10.00
52.00	+10.00
55.00	+10.00
60.00	+10.00
100.00	+10.00
200.00	+10.00

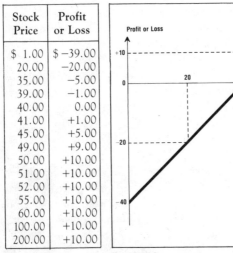

Figure 17   Figure 18

As the Profit/Loss Profile shows, your maximum possible profit in this position would be $10.00 Cdn. You would realize that profit if Seagram moved above $50.00 Cdn. and the call was exercised. It is obvious that you could not possibly make more than $10.00 Cdn. on this position because, when the call was exercised, you would be selling your stock at the exercise price of $50.00 Cdn. instead of the market price, whatever that price may be. By writing the call you severely limited your profit potential.

If Seagram declined, instead of rallying, your profit would start declining as well, until at $40.00 Cdn., you would be breaking even (before commissions). Any decline below $40.00 Cdn. would generate losses, which could conceivably become quite large.

Since you would make a profit if the underlying stock moved up, and incur a loss if it moved far enough down, the strategy of non-simultaneous covered writing is a bullish one. Indeed, if you expected Seagram to decline from its price of $49.50 Cdn. at the time of writing, you should have sold the stock instead of writing a call against it.

Rule 32: NEVER WRITE CALLS AGAINST A STOCK WHICH IS OUTRIGHT BEARISH.

One obvious deficiency of non-simultaneous covered writing is that it is a bullish strategy with limited upside potential and a much larger downside potential. However, things don't look all that bad in our example, since Seagram would have to decline to $40.00 Cdn. before you switched from being a winner to being a loser. And the maximum possible gain of $10.00 Cdn. on a $49.50 Cdn. stock looks impressive enough to consider this strategy seriously, doesn't it?

The correct answer here is: no, the strategy does not look attractive at all. To see why, you have to recall that at the time of writing the April 50 call you already had a profit of $49.50 − $43.00 = $6.50 Cdn. in Seagram. In other words if, instead of writing the call you simply sold the stock, you would have made a profit of $6.50 Cdn. Now it is easy to assess the additional benefit of writing the April 50 call.

All it did for you was to increase your profit potential by $3.50 Cdn., as compared to selling the stock and not writing any calls. Was it worth the risk of losing the profit of $6.50 Cdn.?

My answer is a definite no, because the Reward/Risk Ratio related to this decision is lower than 100%. If you were right and made $10.00 Cdn., instead of $6.50 Cdn., your incremental profit would be equal to $10.00 − $6.50 = $3.50 Cdn. If you were wrong, not only could the entire profit of $6.50 Cdn disappear, but you could end up with a huge loss.

In my opinion, if you did not expect Seagram to rise much higher than $49.50 Cdn., you should have sold the stock and taken a profit. If you hoped for a strong rally to much higher numbers, you should have held the stock, but you should have not written any calls against it so as not to limit the upside potential.

You might reasonably ask me now: why is this strategy among the ones I recommend? The answer is that in a certain special situation, it does make sense to write calls against the stock you own. This situation, however, is quite different from the one described above.

Let us stay with Seagram. On October 5, 1983, you bought 100 shares at $43.00 Cdn. and held it until November 30, 1983, when the stock was trading at $49.50 Cdn. Let us assume that at this time your analysis indicated a strong possibility of a temporary decline. You were still bullish on the stock in the long term, but expected it to weaken before it continued its climb.

Given such circumstances, you sold your shares for $49.50 Cdn. and made a profit of $49.50 − $43.00 = $6.50 Cdn. (before commissions). Your forecast proved to be correct and in a month Seagram declined to $45.00 Cdn. On January 4, 1984, you decided to reinstate your position and bought the stock again at $45.00 Cdn. When Seagram reached $49.50 again, your unrealized profit in it was $49.50 − $45.00 = $4.50 Cdn. Together with the earlier profit of $6.50 Cdn., it brought your total profit to $11.00 Cdn. At this time you were obviously in a better position than if you had not sold Seagram at $49.50 Cdn. and held the stock through the decline and the recovery.

Actually, you could make even more money by not only selling your 100 shares at $49.50 Cdn., but by also selling short another 100 shares at the same time. In that case, on January 4, 1984, you would have closed your short position by buying back 100 shares at $45.00 Cdn., and then reinstated the long position by buying another 100 shares. If you did that, you would have made $49.50 − $45.00 = $4.50 Cdn. on the short position in addition to the $11.00 Cdn. made on the long trades. Your total profit would have been equal to $11.00 + $4.50 = $15.50 Cdn.

What does all that have to do with options? Nothing so far. In this situation, options enter the picture together with the taxman. You will see what I mean if you imagine that instead of buying Seagram at $43.00 Cdn. on October 5, 1983, you bought it many years ago when the stock was much cheaper. Imagine that your cost of the Seagram shares is only $5.50 Cdn., but all the other circumstances are the same, i.e. it is November 30, 1983, Seagram is trading at $49.50 Cdn. and you expect it to decline temporarily to a lower level.

Can you follow all the steps described above? Not really. If you sell your shares or $49.50 Cdn., you will realize a capital gain of $49.50 − $5.50 = $44.00 Cdn. Half of this gain will be taxable, and if you are in the 50% tax bracket, your tax liability will amount to 25% × $44.00 = $11.00 Cdn. Come April, 1984, and you will have to pay to the taxman $11.00 Cdn. per share. Therefore, before you buy any more stocks, you had better put aside $11.00 Cdn. for every share of Seagram sold. Fortunately, it is not a problem, because you have just received $49.50 Cdn. for each share. After you have put aside $11.00 Cdn. per share, all you have left is $49.50 − $11.00 = $38.50 Cdn. per share. So far so good.

The problem arises on January 4, 1984, when you want to buy Seagram back at $45.00 Cdn. You don't have enough money to do that! All you have is $38.50 Cdn. per share, while you need $45.00 Cdn.! In other words, after paying taxes, you do not have enough funds to buy the same number of shares that you held initially. If you expect a major move on the upside in the future, you are better off not to sell at $49.50 Cdn. and not to buy back later at $45.00 Cdn., but to hold the stock through the correction and maintain your initial position.

This is where non-simultaneous covered writing can help you. Instead of selling your Seagram shares for $49.50 Cdn. on November 30, 1983, you should keep the stock and write April 50 calls against it. As I said before, you could receive $3.00 Cdn. per share for these calls.

On January 4, 1984, when Seagram was trading at $45.00 Cdn. and you expected it to rally, you could close the short position in calls by buying them back at $1.00 Cdn. You would have kept your stock intact and you would have also made a profit of $3.00 − $1.00 = $2.00 Cdn. per share. Note that this profit is much smaller than what you could have made by selling the shares and then buying them back:

Rule 30: IN MOST CASES, WRITING CALLS AGAINST THE STOCK AND BUYING THEM BACK WILL YIELD SMALLER PROFITS THAN BUYING AND SELLING THE STOCK ITSELF ON THE SAME DAYS.

However, when you trade options against the stock instead of trading the stock itself, you have to pay taxes only on the profits made in options. In our example, you would be taxed only on the $2.00 Cdn. profit made on the calls. Your main goal of maintaining the entire position in Seagram for further appreciation would have been achieved and a small profit would have been made.

Rule 31: IF YOU WOULD LIKE TO TRADE SHORT-TERM SWINGS IN THE STOCK YOU OWN, BUT YOU CANNOT AFFORD TO SELL THE STOCK BECAUSE OF TAXES, YOU SHOULD TRADE CALL OPTIONS AGAINST THE STOCK.

The above Rule describes *the only situation* in which I recommend writing calls against a long position in the underlying stock.

Once you have decided to write calls against your stock, you are faced with all the same questions as if you were going to write uncovered calls: which calls to write, how to check if the calls are worth writing, when to cover the short position by buying the calls back, etc.

In fact, the similarities with Chapter 6, where uncovered call writing was analyzed, are more than superficial. We can mentally separate the long position in the underlying stock from the short position in the call options. The long position in the stock is bullish. It reflects your bullish sentiment with respect to the stock in the long term. The short position in the calls is bearish. It represents your short-term bearishness with regard to the stock. Looking at your position this way, you can separate the two parts.

You are holding the stock because you are bullish in the long term. Consequently, you do not want to be forced to sell the stock (especially for tax purposes). On the other hand, you expect the stock to decline in the short run, and in order to make some money on that decline, you write calls. Since you do not want to sell the stock, you would like to avoid the exercise of the calls. As a result, you are writing calls with the intention of buying them back at a lower price, which is exactly the same strategy as writing uncovered calls! It is obvious now that all the Rules developed in Chapter 6 for writing uncovered calls are applicable to writing covered calls as well!

First of all, you do not want to write in-the-money calls because they can be exercised any time, and you are trying to avoid exercise at all costs. On the other hand, you do not want to write calls that are too far out-of-the-money, because they are too cheap and do not offer a chance for a decent gain.

Rule 9: WRITE ONLY OUT-OF-THE-MONEY OPTIONS WHICH ARE THE CLOSEST TO BEING AT-THE-MONEY.

Second, the options that are about to expire are also very cheap, but the options which have 6 or more months until expiration are too risky, since they give the underlying stock too much time for a strong rally. Remember, you are bullish on the stock in the long term. If you are right, sooner or later, the stock will run up. At that time, the last thing you need is a short position in calls and a notice that your calls have been exercised!

Rule 10: WRITE ONLY THOSE OPTIONS WHICH HAVE BETWEEN 2 AND 5 MONTHS UNTIL EXPIRATION.

Your profit on writing calls and buying them back cannot be greater than the price of the calls at the time of writing. Therefore, you should never write cheap calls even if they satisfy Rules 9 and 10.

Rule 11: WRITE ONLY THOSE OPTIONS WHOSE PRICE IS AT LEAST 10% OF THE STRIKE PRICE.

One thing you do not have to worry about is a potential take-over. You must remember that for the writer of uncovered calls, there is nothing more dangerous than a take-over or a rumour of such. However, if you own the underlying stock, a take-over will not hurt you. You will miss your chance to make a killing because the calls will be exercised and you will sell the stock at the strike price instead of the take-over price, but you will still end up with a profit. Therefore, a covered writer does not have to check for a possible take-over. If a take-over happens when you have an open short position in calls written against your stock, it will simply mean that your short-term bearish forecast for the stock was a bad one.

Whenever your short-term bearish forecast goes sour and the underlying stock takes off, you should cover the short position in calls before they are exercised:

Rule 14: IF YOUR FORECAST OF THE UNDERLYING STOCK HAS CHANGED UNFAVOURABLY, CLOSE ALL SHORT POSITIONS IMMEDIATELY.

Even if there is no change in the factors determining your bearish forecast, but the underlying stock is rallying, you should cover the short calls. As in the case of uncovered calls, a mental stop-loss is the best tool:

Rule 19: WHEN WRITING CALLS, PLACE A MENTAL STOP-LOSS AT THE PRICE WHICH IS EQUAL TO THE PRICE OF THE UNDERLYING STOCK AT THE TIME OF WRITING PLUS THE PRICE OF THE CALL.

The next logical question is: what to do when your bearish forecast comes true? When should you cover your position in calls? Unfortunately, there is no hard and fast rule in this case, and the comparison with uncovered writing does not help much. When you write uncovered calls, you are outright bearish on the underlying stock. Therefore, as the stock declines, you have nothing to do but wait and watch your profit grow. Rule 13 suggests that you take profits when you can make 75% of the original price of the calls.

The situation is quite different when you are writing against a long position in the underlying stock. In this case, you are not outright bearish. In fact, you are quite bullish long-term but bearish in the short term. Consequently, when the underlying stock declines, you should be ready to play it by ear and to buy the calls back before the decline is reversed. It helps if you have a specific target for the end of the decline. In such a case, you should buy the calls back as soon as the target is reached. If you do not have a specific target, you should buy the calls back as soon as there is a strong enough indication that the decline is over.

Despite all the safeguards, from time to time the calls you have written against the underlying stock will be exercised. Since you like the underlying stock in the long term, you should deliver the shares you own and immediately buy the stock again. However, you should first calculate your tax liability and put aside sufficient funds for paying taxes; then you will be able to determine how many shares of the stock you can afford to buy. Since the actual numbers will depend on your initial cost of the stock and on your tax bracket, there is no rule that would prescribe the number of shares you can buy after the exercise of the calls.

The most important thing to remember about non-simultaneous covered writing is that unless tax considerations make it impossible to sell the stock and buy it back later, you should not write calls against the stock altogether.

Before we move on to the next subject, I would like you to compare Figures 17 and 18 with Figures 3 and 4. Aren't they similar? In both cases, the investor makes a fixed amount of profit when the underlying stock goes up and sustains large losses if the stock declines.

The similarity of the two Profit/Loss Profiles indicates that the two strategies are indeed equivalent. Returning for a moment to our example of Seagram: if you sold the stock at $49.50 Cdn. and wrote an April 50 put for $3.50 Cdn., the Profit/Loss Profile of the resulting position would be exactly the same as if you kept the stock and wrote an April 50 call for $3.00 Cdn.

This is only one of many equivalences existing in options. We will examine these equivalences and the reason for their existence in Chapter 11.

2. Buying Protective Puts

The next strategy, as well as non-simultaneous covered writings, deals with the situation in which the investor owns the underlying stock and uses options in order to increase the profit or to decrease the risk of holding the stock.

Paradoxically, buying puts against the underlying stock is far less popular than writing calls. It is indeed a paradox, because buying puts against the underlying stock is nothing else but buying insurance on the stock! Indeed, the owner of the put has the right to sell the underlying stock at the strike price regardless of the market price of stock at that time. Isn't it a classical example of an insurance contract? When you buy insurance on your house or car, you are guaranteed the payment of a fixed sum of money in case the value of the house or car collapses due to fire, flood, theft, etc. In order to obtain such total protection, you pay certain insurance premiums.

Exactly the same happens when you own a stock and buy puts against it. The puts give you the right to sell the stock at a fixed price. This safeguards you from the possibility of a large loss if the stock goes into a nosedive. Of course, such total protection is not free — you have to pay for the puts you are buying.

The concept of insurance is so widespread that the only asset of a wealthy person that is not usually insured is the stock portfolio! And yet, instead of buying puts against stocks, many investors prefer to write calls. The reason is probably purely historical: calls have been around for much longer than puts and people are more used to them. That is obviously not a valid reason for choosing one investment strategy over another!

Unfortunately, the bias toward writing calls is reflected even in legislation. The only option strategy allowed to pension funds and trust and insurance funds in Canada is covered writing. Buying puts against the same stocks is forbidden as "speculation." The situation is nothing short of ridiculous because writing covered calls still leaves the investor open to a huge loss, while buying protective puts effectively limits the possible loss to a relatively small amount, as you will see from the analysis that follows.

In order to study the Profit/Loss Profile of a protective put (or a put written against a long position in the underlying stock), imagine that you bought 100 shares of Alcan at $26.00 Cdn. in October, 1982. You held the stock until January 9, 1984, when it was trading at $50.50 Cdn. The unrealised profit in your position was equal to $50.50 − $26.00 = $24.50 Cdn. It is only natural that you were tempted to sell the stock and take the profit. The only reason you were not doing it was that you expected the stock to go much higher. You were reluctant to sell and to forego all future profits, but you were also worried about holding the stock through a decline and seeing the profit of $24.50 Cdn. disappear. What could you do in order to lock in the profit and leave some room for future appreciation at the same time?

98

One possible solution was to keep the stock and buy a May 50 put in addition to it. On January 9, 1984, May 50 puts were trading at $2.50 Cdn. Let us analyze the resulting position.

If Alcan rallied to $60.00 Cdn., you would have very little use for the put. Your profit in the stock alone would reach $60.00 − $26.00 = $34.00 Cdn. It would be reduced by the $2.50 Cdn. you paid for the put: $34.00 − $2.50 = $31.50 Cdn.

If Alcan declined to $50.00 Cdn., instead of rallying to $60.00 Cdn., your profit in the stock would amount to $50.00 − $26.00 = $24.00 Cdn. The put would still be useless and the price you paid for it would serve only to reduce your net profit: $24.00 − $2.50 = $21.50 Cdn.

If Alcan declined below $50.00 Cdn., however, you would not even be interested in its actual price. You would exercise the put and, therefore, sell the stock at the strike price of $50.00 Cdn. As calculated above, your net profit would be equal to $21.50 Cdn. The put guaranteed that you could not make less than that!

Repeating similar calculations for various prices of Alcan, we can fill in the table as in Figure 19. The same information can be presented in graph form as in Figure 20:

Stock Price	Profit or Loss
$ 1.00	$ +21.50
20.00	+21.50
40.00	+21.50
49.00	+21.50
50.00	+21.50
51.00	+22.50
52.00	+23.50
55.00	+26.50
60.00	+31.50
80.00	+51.50
100.00	+71.50
200.00	+171.50

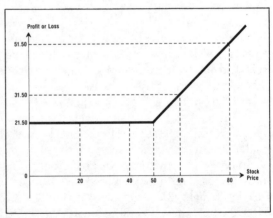

Figure 19   Figure 20

Figures 19 and 20 present an incredibly good looking Profit/Loss Profile! The worst case is making a profit of $21.50 Cdn. Isn't it great?

To put things into perspective, we must not forget that when the position under consideration was taken, there already was a profit of $24.50 Cdn. in Alcan. As Figures 19 and 20 show, this profit can be reduced to $21.50 Cdn., if Alcan declines to or below $50.00 Cdn. On the other hand, the upside potential is unlimited. However, all the profits that can be made on the stock will be reduced by the $2.50 Cdn. paid for the put.

When investors first discover this strategy and realise its similarity to buying insurance, they usually decide to use it as often as possible. Indiscriminate use of this strategy, however, will not improve the performance of your portfolio in the long run. On one hand, your losses will be much smaller than without writing puts. On the other hand, the cost of the puts will bite right into your profits. They key to the success of this strategy is to buy protective puts only when they are cheap.

The next obvious question is: what is cheap? In order to answer it, we will avoid developing a new set of Rules. Instead, we will use a particular equivalence, which will allow us to use the Rules already analyzed in the previous chapters.

Let us go back to January 9, 1984. Alcan is trading at $50.50 Cdn. and you are considering the purchase of a May 50 put. Imagine now that instead of buying that put, you sold your 100 shares of Alcan for $50.50 Cdn. and simultaneously bought a May 50 call at its market price of $4.50 Cdn. What kind of Profit/Loss Profile would such a position give you?

First of all, you have made a profit of $24.50 Cdn. on the stock. The shares are sold and nothing can happen to that profit.

If Alcan declines to or below $50.00 Cdn., your call would become worthless. Its cost would then reduce your profit to $24.50 − $4.50 = $20.00 Cdn.

If Alcan rallies to $60.00 Cdn., your May 50 call will be worth at least $60.00 − $50.00 = $10.00 Cdn. The net profit on the call alone would be equal to $10.00 − $4.50 = $5.50 Cdn. This profit would, of course, be added to the profit of $24.50 Cdn. on the stock, which would result in the total net profit of $24.50 + $5.50 = $30.00 Cdn.

Repeating similar calculations for different prices of Alcan, we can fill in the table as in Figure 21. The same information can be presented in graph form as in Figure 22.

If you compare Figures 19 and 20 with Figures 21 and 22, you will notice that they are almost identical. The only difference between the two is that at any price of Alcan the strategy of selling the stock and buying a call would yield a profit which would be $1.50 Cdn. less than the profit achieved at the same price of Alcan by the strategy of keeping the stock and buying a protective put.

The existence of this difference is easy to explain. If you kept the stock and bought a put, you would continue to receive dividends on the stock. If you sold the stock and bought a call, you would stop receiving dividends, but you would free a relatively large amount of cash. This cash would earn interest at a rate much higher than that applicable to dividends. The difference between the amount of

Stock Price	Profit or Loss
$ 1.00	$ +20.00
20.00	+20.00
40.00	+0.00
49.00	+20.00
50.00	+20.00
51.00	+21.00
52.00	+22.00
55.00	+25.00
60.00	+30.00
80.00	+50.00
100.00	+70.00
200.00	+170.00

Figure 21   **Figure 22**

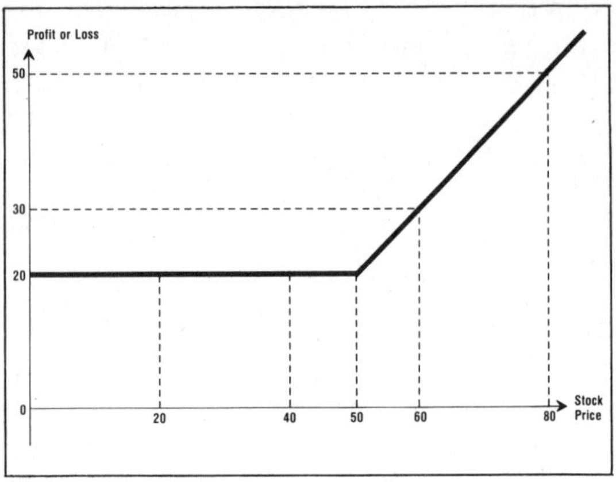

interest you could receive on free cash and the amount of dividends you could receive on the stock would be equal to the $1.50 Cdn. difference in the Profit/Loss Profiles of the two strategies.

Now it is obvious that the two strategies are completely identical. This is another equivalence which will be explained and analyzed in Chapter 11. At this point we know enough about it to use it in analyzing the strategy of writing protective puts. Indeed, if writing protective puts against a long position in the underlying stock is completely equivalent to selling the stock and buying calls, all we have to do is analyze the feasibility of buying calls. Consequently, we do not need any new Rules. You can simply follow all the Rules presented in Chapter 5 for buying calls!

Rule 33: YOU SHOULD BUY PUTS AGAINST A LONG POSITION IN THE UNDERLYING STOCK ONLY IF YOU COULD SELL THE STOCK AND BUY CORRESPONDING CALLS WITHOUT VIOLATING ANY OF THE RULES APPLICABLE TO CALLS. (TAX CONSIDERATIONS MIGHT PROVIDE EXCEPTIONS TO THIS RULE.)

In the case of Alcan, in order to see if writing May 50 puts against the stock was a good idea, you had to imagine that you sold the stock first and were considering buying May 50 calls. You had to check all the Rules applicable to buying calls with regard to Alcan May 50 calls. If all the Rules confirmed that the purchase of May 50 calls was indeed a good strategy, then buying May 50 puts against the stock was also a good strategy.

Another interesting application for the strategy of buying protective puts is based on index options. In recent years various Exchanges have listed options that are based on broad stock market indices rather than individual stocks. We will discuss these options further in Chapter 12, but this is a good time to mention the strategy of protecting your portfolio by buying index puts.

If you have a large, diversified portfolio of stocks, you might be reluctant to liquidate it completely when you expect a short-term weakness in the stock market. Of course, you should liquidate if the market seems to be ready to turn bearish in the long term. But if you are bullish in the long term and expect a short-term correction, liquidating the entire portfolio and re-accumulating it at a later day might be too cumbersome and too costly from the commissions standpoint. Most investors simply keep their stocks and watch them decline and later return to the previous high levels.

You can do better than that. You can buy protective puts, and instead of buying these puts against each stock in your portfolio, you can buy them on a market index such as S&P 100 or S&P 500. This would have several advantages over buying puts on every stock you own.

First, not all stocks in your portfolio might be optionable. Second, the cost in commissions is much lower if you buy calls on the index and take a relatively large position, rather than buying many smaller positions on individual stocks. Third, if you have been paying due attention to stock selection, the stocks in your portfolio would decline less in the average than a broad market index. Therefore, buying puts on the index would yield higher profit on the puts themselves than buying puts on your superior stocks.

When you think that the correction is over, you would buy the puts on the index back and keep the stocks. The profit on the puts would partially offset the decline in the value of stocks in your portfolio.

You might have noticed that Rule 33 mentions some exceptions related to taxes. Indeed, buying puts against a stock can be a very powerful tool for deferring taxes. In order to illustrate this concept, imagine that you bought 500 shares of Bell Canada at $19.00 Cdn. in September, 1982. Slightly over a year later, on November 30, 1983, the stock was trading at $33.50 Cdn. You had a nice unrealised profit of $33.50 − $19.00 = $14.50 Cdn. Your analysis indicated that the upside potential of the stock was limited and that it could very easily top out and undergo a downside correction. Given this information, you were ready to sell Bell Canada and to use the money elsewhere. The only thing that was stopping you from calling your broker immediately was that if you sold the shares on November 30, 1983, you would have to pay taxes on the gain in April, 1984. On the other hand, if you could hold the shares for another month and sell them in January, 1984, the taxes on the gain would become payable only in April, 1985. Yet you were not prepared to hold the shares until January and to take a chance that Bell Canada would indeed decline and wipe out some of the profit.

Buying protective puts could solve your problem. You could keep the shares and buy 5 February 35 puts at $2.00 Cdn. Then you could calmly wait for January. If Bell Canada declined more than $2.00 Cdn. before the expiration of the puts, you would exercise them and sell the stock at $35.00 Cdn. Your profit would be reduced by the $2.00 Cdn. paid for the puts, but your taxes would not be payable until April, 1985.

If Bell Canada remained at more or less the same level, you would sell both the stock and the puts at the beginning of January, 1984. Your taxes would be deferred for a year and your loss on the puts would be reduced by whatever you could get for them at that time.

If Bell Canada rallied to new highs, you would still sell the stock and the puts, and the additional profit on the stock would cover the loss on the puts. The taxes would still be deferred.

The same tax deferral technique can be used by the U.S. investors who would like to hold a stock for a few weeks longer in order to convert a would be short-term gain into a long-term one.

Rule 34: IF YOU WOULD LIKE TO HOLD A RISKY STOCK SEVERAL WEEKS LONGER FOR TAX PURPOSES, CONSIDER BUYING PUTS AGAINST IT.

When you are buying protective puts in order to defer taxes, you might decide to buy the puts that are somewhat more expensive than Rule 33 suggests. How much more you are prepared to pay for the puts, which offer you a tax deferral, is a matter of taste. It pays to remember that you are not eliminating the tax liability altogether. You are only postponing it for a year. Consequently, you should not buy protective puts if they are prohibitively expensive, even for tax purposes. It is up to you to assign a value to the tax deferral and to assess the price of a protective put.

3. Replacing Stock With Calls

In the previous section, we analyzed the strategy of buying protective puts, i.e. buying puts against a long position in the underlying stock. One reason for doing that was to defer the sale of the stock and therefore to defer the payment of taxes on the gain in the stock. The protective put provided insurance against a sudden decline in the price of the stock as the owner was waiting for January of the next year.

In this section we will be dealing with the opposite idea — selling the stock and buying calls to replace the sold shares. If we tried to apply this strategy to the example of Bell Canada, used in the previous section, we would receive rather disappointing results. By selling the stock we would immediately incur a tax liability, which was the opposite to our intentions. So why would an investor want to replace a stock with calls?

The reason is as simple as it is sad. Stocks do not always make spectacular gains for the benefit of their owners. Sometimes quite the opposite happens.

Mitel has recently provided a perfect illustration. In January, 1983, it was proudly trading at $38.00 Cdn. Since for every seller there is a buyer, some terribly unlucky investors actually bought Mitel at that price. For the next ten months, these investors must have felt like someone going over Niagara Falls in an inflatable dingy!

On November 30, 1983, Mitel was trading at $15.00 Cdn. At that time the investor who bought the stock at $38.00 Cdn. faced a dilemma. He had an unrealized loss of $38.00 − $15.00 = $23.00 Cdn. and he was definitely tempted to sell the unhappy stock, to take the loss and to use it in the 1984 tax return. Many investors, however, felt that $15.00 Cdn. was the rock bottom for Mitel. They expected the stock to base and to start climbing back up.

If there is anything an investor hates more than buying at the top, it is selling at the bottom. After having bought at $38.00 Cdn., many holders of Mitel would never forgive themselves for selling at $15.00 Cdn., if it happened to be the bottom. They could just see their egos shattered, their reputations destroyed, their hair turning grey and falling out, their professional careers going down the drain. . . There is no self-torture severe enough for a market player who bought at the top and then sold at the bottom!

This is where options offer a graceful and logical way out. By selling the Mitel shares for $15.00 Cdn. on November 30, 1983, and immediately buying a corresponding number of March 15 calls at $1.80 Cdn. the owner of the stock could realize his taxable loss and still maintain some exposure to the stock. Indeed, if $15.00 Cdn. were indeed a bottom and if Mitel proceeded to stage a strong rally, the investor would simply exercise the calls and buy the same number of shares of Mitel at $15.00 Cdn. Of course, all his future profits would be reduced by the $1.80 Cdn. he paid for the calls (there is no free lunch!).

In addition to providing exposure to the stock in case of a rally, the calls offer limited risk. As it happened, Mitel did not bottom out at $15.00 Cdn. It just took a brief pause and then plunged further. By July, 1984, the stock had declined to $5.25 Cdn.! Anyone who continued holding Mitel in November, 1983, instead of replacing it with calls, would have sustained further losses far in excess of the $1.80 Cdn. asked for the calls.

Rule 35: IF YOU EXPECT A QUICK RECOVERY IN THE STOCK WHICH YOU OTHERWISE WOULD HAVE SOLD FOR TAX PURPOSES, SELL THE STOCK AND BUY CALLS.

American investors can use the same technique in order to accelerate the recognition of losses before they become of a long-term nature.

4. Fixing Stock Price Until Funds Are Available

As you have already seen, options provide a great variety of strategies compared to buying and selling stocks. For example, buying calls or puts, as well as writing uncovered calls or puts, can be done instead of buying stocks or selling them short. Buying or writing straddles and combinations allows the investor to capitalize on an expected change in the volatility of the stock. Non-simultaneous covered writing, buying protective puts and replacing a stock with calls, can offer various tax advantages not available without the use of options.

The strategy we are going to analyze in this section is very useful in a situation in which you would like to buy a stock immediately, but you do not have enough free funds. However, in a relatively short future such funds will become available. The problem is that if you wait for the funds to be received, the price of the stock might be much higher than when you have just made the decision to buy it.

Such situations arise when you expect to receive a large bonus, a large commission cheque, a payment on sold property, the repayment of principle amount upon the maturity of a bond, etc. In every case, you know in advance the amount and the date of the expected receipt, which helps you to plan and to devise an appropriate option strategy.

Imagine that on September 21, 1984, you were very bullish on Dupont. The stock was trading at $49.50 US and you were completely ready to buy 1000 shares at that price. The only obstacle in your way was the sad fact that you did not have $49,000.00 US available. Nor did you have half of that amount which would allow you to buy Dupont on margin. In fact, all you could spare was

$3,000.00 US. However, you expected to receive over $50,000.00 US in two months.

Of course, you could simply sit and wait until you received your cheque and buy the stock then. But such a course of action did not appeal to you in the least. Your analysis indicated that the stock was grossly undervalued and that a strong rally could start at any time. You hated the idea of missing such a move and of watching helplessly how other people were getting rich when you were the one who knew about the upcoming move. You wanted to act immediately.

One way in which you could achieve your goal was to buy 10 January 50 calls, which were trading at $2.50 US on September 21, 1984. These calls gave you the right to buy 1000 shares of Dupont at $50.00 US at any time before expiration. Of course, any future profit would then be reduced by the $2.50 US paid for the calls. Such was the price of the manoeuvre (remember, there is no free lunch!). Buying January 50 calls would allow you to fix the purchase price of Dupont at $50.00 + $2.50 = $52.50 US until expiration in January.

Rule 36: IF YOU WOULD LIKE TO BUY A STOCK BUT THE FUNDS WILL BECOME AVAILABLE ONLY SEVERAL MONTHS LATER, CONSIDER BUYING CALLS IN ORDER TO FIX THE PRICE OF THE STOCK.

Of course, the price of the calls is very important in making the decision to use this strategy. If, in our example, you expected Dupont to move only one or two dollars before you received your cheque, you should not have purchased the calls. On the other hand, if you expected a move larger than $3.00 US, then the purchase of the calls certainly made a lot of sense.

Another factor to consider is the timing of the exercise. Let us say that you did buy the calls and that, by the time you received your big cheque, the stock has moved up so far that exercising the calls makes sense. Should you exercise immediately?

There is no hard and fast answer to this question.

If you exercise immediately, you will acquire the stock and start receiving dividends (if the stock pays such). If you do not exercise immediately, you will receive no dividends, but the received cash will earn interest. In order to make the best decision you have to compare the amount of interest you can receive on your free cash with the amount of dividend you can receive on the stock:

Rule 37: IF YOU INTEND TO PURCHASE A STOCK BY EXERCISING CALLS AND IF THE INTEREST ON THE CASH IS

GREATER THAN THE DIVIDENDS ON THE STOCK, DO IT ON
THE EXPIRATION DAY.

Chapter 9

Non-Recommended Strategies
1. Simultaneous Covered Writing
2. Writing Calls To Sell Stock
3. Writing Puts To Buy Stock
4. Spreads

In this chapter we will discuss several popular strategies that I do not recommend under any circumstances. The reason for such a categoric denial is not that these strategies never generate any profits. If they didn't, they would not have been so popular. The reason for my negative opinion on these strategies is that, even under the best conditions, they are inferior to other strategies. We have already analyzed the most effective strategies in Chapter 8; now is the time to show why many other popular strategies produce inferior results. Let us start with covered writing.

1. Simultaneous Covered Writing

You might remember from our earlier discussions that simultaneous covered writing consists of buying a stock and simultaneously writing calls against it. Another popular name for this strategy is "buy-writing." The origins of the strategy can be found in the natural desire of investors to buy stocks as cheaply as possible. The logic is simple: if you buy a stock and at the same time write calls against it, the proceeds from the sale of the calls will reduce the purchase price of the stock. Simple and elegant, isn't it?

The main problem of bargain-hunters is that they try to defy the basic law of Nature, which states that there is no free lunch. If you are getting something cheaper than its regular price, there is a reason for it. For example, it is quite all right to buy a fur coat in April at a 25% discount. The timing of the purchase explains the reduction in price. If the same coat is offered at the same discount in October, however, a shrewd consumer would be right to suspect that there is something wrong with it.

The same rule applies to investments. We always try to find

investments that are "cheap" relative to our expectations of their prices in the future. Yet we should never jump into something just because it looks cheap. There might be a very good reason for the low price. Only when we know something that others don't, can we afford to buy securities at low prices and then wait until everybody discovers what we have known all along. Such is not the case with simultaneous covered writing.

In order to discover the real "price" of buying stocks cheaper through simultaneous covered writing, let us examine the Profit/Loss Profile of this strategy. Imagine that on September 25, 1984, you bought 1000 shares of Northern Telecom at $50.00 Cdn. At the same time you wrote 10 January 50 calls for $4.00 Cdn.

If you deduct the $4.00 Cdn. that you received for the calls from the $50.00 Cdn. that you paid for the stock, you would conclude that the net cost of the transaction was $46.00 Cdn. So far your thinking would be flawless. However, if you proceeded to conclude that you had fooled Mother Nature and had bought Northern Telecom $4.00 Cdn. cheaper than its market price, you would have been totally wrong.

Indeed, if Northern Telecom rallied above $50.00 Cdn. and stayed there until expiration, your calls would be exercised. This would force you to sell the shares for the strike price of $50.00 Cdn. The only profit you would have made would be the $4.00 Cdn. received for the calls. Even if the stock ran up to $100.00 Cdn., you would still have to settle for a $4.00 Cdn. profit!

On the other hand, if Northern Telecom declined to, say, $40.00 Cdn., the calls would expire worthless and you would keep the $4.00 Cdn. received for them. But this amount would not be sufficient to eliminate the loss of $50.00 − $40.00 = $10.00 Cdn. on the stock. It would only reduce the loss to $10.00 − $4.00 = $6.00 Cdn.

Repeating similar calculations for various prices of Northern Telecom, we can fill in the table as in Figure 23. The same information can be presented in graph form as in Figure 24.

Now you can clearly see why simultaneous covered writing does not help the investor to fool Nature. The mere fact of having calls written against the stock robs the investor of most of the upside potential! In exchange, the calls offer limited protection on the downside by reducing potential losses on the stock by the amount received for the calls.

So far we have dispersed one myth about simultaneous covered writing — that it allows you to buy the underlying stock below the market price. When you pay less than the market price, you receive something different from the underlying stock. It is as simple as that.

Stock Price	Profit or Loss
$ 1.00	$ −45.00
20.00	−26.00
40.00	−6.00
45.00	−1.00
46.00	−0.00
47.00	+1.00
48.00	+2.00
49.00	+3.00
50.00	+4.00
51.00	+4.00
55.00	+4.00
60.00	+4.00
80.00	+4.00
100.00	+4.00
200.00	+4.00

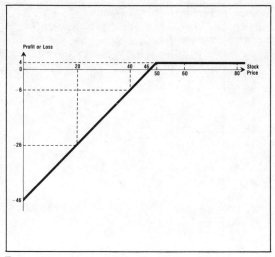

Figure 23   Figure 24

After many years of experimentation, investors have realized what is so obvious on Figures 23 and 24, i.e. that covered writing cannot be used as a way of "discounting" the price of the underlying stock. Yet many of them did not give up on simultaneous covered writing altogether. Instead, they started using it as a separate strategy, which was a major step forward.

The new approach to simultaneous covered writing was based on the fact that from time to time calls become very expensive. For example, it often happens after a strong rally in the underlying stock. The more expensive the calls relative to the stock, the more protection they provide on the downside and the more room is left for profits on the upside. In other words, the pricier the calls, the better the Reward/Risk Ratio of the simultaneous covered writer.

Doesn't it mean that at a certain level of call prices the strategy would begin to make sense? The answer is a definite yes. So why do I not recommend it?

Simply because there is a better way to achieve the same result.

Returning to our example of Northern Telecom; instead of buying 1000 shares at $50.00 Cdn. and writing 10 January 50 calls for $4.00 Cdn. on September 25, 1984, you could write 10 January 50 puts for $2.50 Cdn. on the same day. The strategy of writing uncovered puts has been analyzed in Chapter 5. If you repeat all the steps outlined in that chapter for building the Profit/Loss Profile of a short put, you will obtain the result as in Figure 25. The same information can be presented in graph form as in Figure 26:

110

Stock Price	Profit or Loss
$ 1.00	$ −46.50
20.00	−27.50
40.00	−7.50
45.00	−2.50
46.00	−1.50
47.00	−0.50
47.50	+0.00
48.00	+0.50
49.00	+1.50
50.00	+2.50
51.00	+2.50
55.00	+2.50
60.00	+2.50
80.00	+2.50
100.00	+2.50
200.00	+2.50

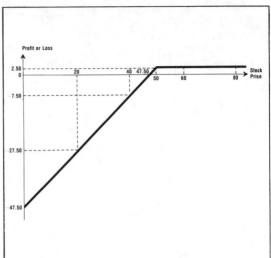

Figure 25   Figure 26

If you compare Figures 25 and 26 with Figures 23 and 24, you will realize that we are dealing with yet another equivalence. At any price of Northern Telecom, the profit or loss generated by an uncovered short put is $1.50 Cdn. different from the profit or loss generated by simultaneous covered writing. In other words, the writer of the puts is always $1.50 worse off than the simultaneous covered writer. That is, until we consider interest and dividends.

The simultaneous covered writer had to pay $46.00 Cdn. per share for his position. 1000 shares would cost him $46,000.00 Cdn. before commissions. Since the owner of his position actually owned the stock, he would be receiving dividends.

The writer of the puts, on the other hand, did not have to pay for his position. Even though he would have to post a certain margin, this margin would still be invested as a cash deposit and would, therefore, earn interest. The general level of interest rates in November, 1984, was much higher than the rate at which Northern Telecom paid dividends. The difference, calculated on a per share basis, was equal exactly to $1.50 Cdn. In other words, simultaneous covered writing is equivalent to writing uncovered puts.

This still does not explain why I do not recommend simultaneous covered writing while I do recommend writing uncovered puts. The reasons have to do with practical considerations rather than the Profit/Loss Profile.

First, buying a stock and writing calls is much more expensive than writing puts from the commission standpoint. Second, simultaneous covered writing requires simultaneous action in two different markets, since stocks and options on them are handled by different floor traders. In the United States, options are traded on different Exchanges from the underlying stocks, which makes the simultaneous execution even more difficult. By contrast, writing puts requires only one action by one floor trader and is, therefore, much easier to execute.

Rule 38: WRITING PUTS IS ALWAYS PREFERABLE TO SIMULTANEOUS COVERED WRITING.

The obvious exception from this Rule are those investors who are not allowed to engage in writing puts. Such limitations exist for many pension funds and trust companies. As our analysis has proven, the limitation is totally unreasonable, since writing puts cannot possibly be riskier or more speculative than simultaneous covered writing. Unfortunately, until the rulemakers educate themselves sufficiently to realize that the two strategies are completely equivalent, pension funds and trust companies will continue to be forced to use simultaneous covered writing when the best possible course of action would be writing uncovered puts.

Before we leave simultaneous covered writing and move on to other strategies, I would like to deal with two more myths. The first one has to do with the popular belief that simultaneous covered writing is a "neutral" strategy. Figures 23 and 24 clearly show that it is not true. A simultaneous covered writer makes money when the underlying stock advances, and loses money when the stock declines. Therefore, the strategy is definitely bullish rather than neutral.

The second myth states that a simultaneous covered writer "locks in" a certain rate of return on his investment. This myth is so popular that some option professionals compare simultaneous covered writing with buying money market instruments. In fact, nothing could be further from the truth. One look at Figures 23 and 24 is sufficient to realize that there is no fixed rate of return on investment guaranteed to a simultaneous covered writer. On the contrary, there is a definite possibility of losses which can be quite substantial. If somebody ever tells you that by writing calls and buying stock you can lock in a profit or a rate of return, always ask such an adviser what will happen if the stock declines by 50%. This question puts a quick end to all mythical claims about simultaneous covered writing.

2. Writing Calls To Sell Stock

We have already analyzed and discussed non-simultaneous covered writing in Chapter 8. All I want to do here is to present another example that illustrates why I am opposed to it, given a different objective.

Imagine that you bought 100 shares of General Motors at $62.00 US in June, 1984, and held them until September 21, 1984, when the stock was trading at $76.00 US.

At that point you were not sure if you should sell the stock or hold it for a run to $80.00 US. On one hand, you had a profit of $76.00 − $62.00 = $14.00 US in the stock, which translated into a 23% gain in only 3 months. On the other hand, your analysis indicated that the stock could easily climb up to $80.00 US. You were torn between fear and greed (which is a normal state of every market player). You were afraid to lose the unrealized profit of $14.00 US if General Motors declined and you wanted to see your profit grow if the stock did, in fact, rally up to $80.00 US.

One possible alternative was to write a March 75 call against the stock, which you could do for $6.00 US. The idea could seem attractive because writing the call would provide additional cash inflow of $6.00 US. If the call was subsequently exercised, you would be selling the stock for $75.00 US, which together with the $6.00 US gave you a profit of $75.00 + $6.00 − $62.00 = $19.00 US. This profit would be larger than the $14.00 US which you could realize by selling the stock immediately instead of writing calls. Another attractive feature was the fact that the $6.00 US received for the call seemed to cushion a possible decline in the stock.

Unfortunately, both attractive features have flaws. It is true that if the calls were exercised, you would make a larger profit than by selling the stock on September 21, 1984 for $76.00 US. The calls would be exercised, however, only if the stock remained above $75.00 US. One possible way of staying above $75.00 US is to rally up to a much higher number. If General Motors ran up to, say, $90.00 US, you could not take advantage of such a development because your call would be exercised.

On the other hand, if General Motors declined (as it actually did), you could not use the entire $6.00 US received for the call to cushion the fall. As soon as you sold the stock, you would have to buy back the call in order not to end up with an uncovered short call. The price you would have to pay for the call would reduce the cushioning effect.

The conclusion is very simple. If you believe strongly enough that there is further potential in the stock you own, you should hold it without writing calls against it. If you are not sure that you should keep holding the stock, sell it and still don't write any calls.

Rule 39: WRITING CALLS AGAINST A STOCK IS NOT A GOOD WAY TO SELL THE STOCK.

It might seem contradictory that I recommended non-simultaneous covered writing in Chapter 8 and I am advising you not to use it in Chapter 9. Indeed, the strategy under consideration is exactly the same as far as the transactions are concerned: first you buy a stock, then you wait, then you write calls against it. What is different, however, is the intent. In Chapter 8, I recommended writing covered calls in order to defer income taxes. Here I suggest that writing calls against a stock is not a good way to sell the stock. The instrument which is good for one task is not necessarily appropriate for another. In other words, it is not what you do, but why you are doing it, that defines a strategy and its merit.

3. Writing Puts To Buy Stock

Bargain hunters do not give up easily. As soon as they figured out that simultaneous covered writing was not a good way to buy stocks, they devised another plot. Instead of writing calls against the stock, they started writing uncovered puts.

Let us say that a bargain hunter by the name of Mr. Cheap was bullish on Bow Valley Industries and was contemplating the purchase of the stock at $19.50 Cdn. on July 20, 1984. The only thing that prevented Mr. Cheap from placing an order right away was his cherished habit of buying everything below the retail price. In other words, he wanted a bargain.

Previous experience had taught Mr. Cheap not to write calls against the stock he was buying. Therefore, he tried another trick on Bow Valley Industries. Instead of buying the stock, he wrote January 20 puts for $1.80 Cdn. His rationale was very simple. Since the puts were in-the-money, he expected them to be exercised. Upon exercise, he would buy the stock at the strike price of $20.00 Cdn. and he would still keep the $1.80 Cdn. received for the puts. His net cost would then be equal to $20.00 − $1.80 = $18.20 Cdn., which was $1.30 Cdn. cheaper than the market price of $19.50 Cdn. on July 20, 1984.

Mr. Cheap was very proud of his plot. Unfortunately for him, this blissful state did not last for long. Two weeks after the day of the transaction, Bow Valley Industries was trading above $25.00 Cdn. The puts that Mr. Cheap wrote had not been exercised and, therefore, he did not own a single share of Bow Valley Industries. Instead of a profit of over \$5.00 Cdn. on the stock, he had to settle for a profit of \$1.80 Cdn. on the puts.

Mr. Cheap learned a very important lesson. As a writer of puts, he had no control over exercising of the puts. He had to wait for the owner of the puts to exercise them before he could buy the stock at the strike price. If Bow Valley Industries remained below \$20.00 Cdn. long enough, the puts would be exercised for certain. However, Mr. Cheap was right about the bullish prospects for the stock, and as soon as the stock moved up, the puts became out-of-the-money and, therefore, were not exercised.

Of course, when the rally started, Mr. Cheap could buy the stock at, say, \$21.00 Cdn. and still keep the short position in the puts. However, he would then have to consider the possibility of a sudden decline in the price of Bow Valley Industries and a sudden exercise of his puts. If that happened, he would end up buying twice as many shares of Bow Valley as he originally intended: one position would have been bought in the market at \$21.00 Cdn. and the second one through the exercise of the puts at \$20.00 Cdn. Since Mr. Cheap was not prepared to buy twice as many as what he had in mind originally, this alternative had to be rejected.

And yet Mr. Cheap did not give up. He had another idea. What if he kept writing puts as the underlying stock moved up? It seemed to him that either he would end up buying the stock below the market, or he would make a lot more money than by writing puts only once.

He discussed this plan with his good old friend Mrs. Miser, who was also an avid market player. What Mrs. Miser said surprised Mr. Cheap. She asked him not to try out his new strategy until they had lunch.

When the two got together a few days later, Mrs. Miser did not carry one of the tiny purses that she usually favoured. Instead, she brought with her a fat, vinyl attaché case, from which she produced a stack of trading slips dating back to 1982. At the sight of the slips, Mr. Cheap guessed that his old friend had already tried the strategy of writing puts on a rising stock. The way Mrs. Miser threw the slips on the table told Mr. Cheap that she was less than pleased with the results.

Mr. Cheap was absolutely correct. The slips showed that on August 13, 1982, Mrs. Miser wrote February 35 puts on Raytheon for \$3.00 US. At that time the stock was trading at \$35.00 US and looked very promising. Mrs. Miser hoped that Raytheon would decline for a brief period, the puts would be exercised, and she would buy the stock through the exercise at \$35.00 US and would also keep the \$3.00 US received for the puts. If all that worked out, her net cost would be equal to \$35.00 − \$3.00 = \$32.00 US.

As it happened, Raytheon quickly ran up to $46.00 US, hesitated for a while at that level, and then corrected down to $41.00 US. On September 30, 1982, Mrs. Miser became thoroughly convinced that the stock was not about to decline all the way to $35.00 US. She bought back her February 35 puts at $1.25 US and immediately wrote February 40 puts for $2.75 US. Her profit on February 35 puts amounted to $3.00 − $1.25 = $1.75 US.

These puts were not exercised either. Raytheon rallied to the high of $49.88 in October, 1982, and then came back all the way to $38.62 US in November, 1982. As the stock dipped below $40.00 US, Mrs. Miser kept her long-nailed fingers crossed in hope that the puts would be exercised. Alas, they were not. The only reason Mrs. Miser escaped having her fingers permanently cramped was because Raytheon spent the total of three days below $40.00 US and then moved up once more. By December, 1982, the stock was trading above $48.00 US, and the next correction bottomed at $42.25 US. The stock started climbing again and reached $46.00 US on January 7, 1983.

At this point, Mrs. Miser gave up hope of buying Raytheon below $40.00 US and bought back her February 40 puts at $0.75 US. Since she was still bullish on the stock, she immediately wrote May 45 puts for $3.25 US. In the process, she made a profit of $2.75 − $0.75 = $2.00 US on February 40 puts.

Raytheon continued climbing. By March 25, 1983, it reached $53.00 US, and Mrs. Miser's analysis indicated that there was not much more bullish potential in the stock. Consequently, she bought back her May 45 puts at $0.12 US for a profit of $3.25 − $0.12 = $3.13 US.

The total profit of Mrs. Miser was equal to $1.75 + $2.00 + $3.13 = $6.88 US. There is nothing wrong with making a profit, but if she had bought Raytheon at $35.00 US on August 13, 1982, held it until March 25, 1983, and sold it then for $53.50 US, she would have made $53.50 − $35.00 = $18.50 US plus some dividends! A simple strategy of buying and holding the stock would have brought a profit almost three times larger than chasing the stock with short puts! If Mrs. Miser traded Raytheon's short-term swings instead of holding it, she could have made even higher profits.

Rule 40: WRITING UNCOVERED PUTS IS NOT A GOOD WAY TO BUY THE UNDERLYING STOCK.

In Chapter 5, I recommended writing uncovered puts as a bullish strategy to be used when the calls are too expensive. In this section, I recommend avoiding writing uncovered puts as a means of buying the underlying stock. As we have already discussed, the same type of transaction (i.e. writing uncovered puts) can be a good strategy or a bad one, depending on the intent of the writer.

Here is a super-brief summary of the last two sections of this chapter:

IF YOU LIKE THE STOCK, BUY IT!

4. Spreads

"A Spread" is a name for a position that combines either long and short calls or long and short puts. If you buy various calls and write various other calls, the resulting position will be called *a call spread.* Depending on which calls you bought and which ones you wrote, you might end up with a *bullish* or *bearish* call spread, *vertical* or *calendar* call spread. If you use puts instead of calls and buy and write various puts at the same time, you will own *a put spread.* Depending on the puts bought and written, this spread can also be *bullish, bearish, vertical,* or *calendar.* However, there are no spreads that combine calls and puts.

Since there is no limit to the number of possible combinations of calls or puts, there is also a theoretically infinite number of possible spreads. Fortunately, only a very small number of spreads have received enough publicity to become popular. The reason is simple. The more different calls or puts you jam into one position, the more commissions you will have to pay in order to establish or close such a position. As a matter of fact, commission costs make any position that requires more than two series of calls or puts prohibitively expensive.

One good example is "a butterfly spread" which involves three different series of calls. A friend of mine, after having tried to catch a few of these "butterflies," has relabeled them "crocodile spreads." I must admit that the latter is a much better name, because the commissions one has to pay on the way in and out of such a spread eat all the potential profits before these profits get a chance to be born!

If you are beginning to feel that I am not in love with those fancy spreads, you are absolutely correct. If you also have a vague suspicion that I do not like any spreads, you are right again. In fact, I have only one Rule to offer with regard to spreading:

Rule 41: DO NOT USE SPREADS.

It is probably the simplest Rule in the entire book!

In order to illustrate this Rule, I will show you some of the most popular spreads and the problems associated with them. If you ever come across a spread that is not covered in this section, you will still be able to analyze it in the same manner as the spreads presented below and discover for yourself all the problems related to that spread.

Let us start with *a vertical bullish call spread*. A *vertical* spread is the one in which the expiry months of all the calls or puts involved is the same.

On August 17, 1984, Imperial Oil was trading at $38.50 Cdn. on the Toronto Stock Exchange. On the same day Mr. Fancy, a devoted spread player, established a vertical bullish call spread by buying 5 Imperial Oil February 35 calls and simultaneously writing 5 Imperial Oil February 40 calls. He paid $5.25 Cdn. for the February 35 calls and received $2.50 Cdn. for the February 40 calls. His net cost per share was $5.25 − $2.50 = $2.75 Cdn.

Let us build the Profit/Loss Profile of this position.

If Imperial Oil falls below $35.00 Cdn. and remains there until expiration, both series of calls become worthless. In that case, Mr. Fancy would lose whatever he paid, i.e. $2.75 Cdn. per share.

If Imperial Oil remained at $38.50 Cdn. until expiration, February 40 calls would expire without being exercised. Consequently, Mr. Fancy would get to keep the money he received for them. On the other hand, February 35 calls would be worth exactly $38.50 − $35.00 = $3.50 Cdn. By selling them for this price, Mr. Fancy would not only have recovered his investment, but he would also make a profit of $3.50 − $2.75 = $0.75 Cdn.

If the stock rallied to $50.00 Cdn., February 40 calls would acquire an intrinsic value of $50.00 − $40.00 = $10.00 Cdn. They would be exercised and Mr. Fancy would find himself short 500 shares of Imperial Oil and the price of $40.00 Cdn. At that moment he would have two alternatives. Either he could buy the stock in the market at $50.00 Cdn. and cover the short position, or he could exercise his February 35 calls and therefore buy 500 shares of the stock at $35.00 Cdn., which would also cover his short position. Obviously, the second alternative is much more attractive.

By buying Imperial Oil at $35.00 Cdn. and selling it at $40.00 Cdn., Mr. Fancy would make a profit of $40.00 − $35.00 = $5.00 Cdn. on the stock. His net profit would be equal to $5.00 − $2.75 = $2.25 Cdn.

In practice, option players always try to avoid the exercise of their short options in order to avoid commissions on buying and selling the underlying stock. If Imperial Oil was trading at $50.00 Cdn. a few weeks before expiration, Mr. Fancy would simply buy back 5 February

40 calls and sell his 5 February 35 calls. Since at the time, both series of calls would be trading very close to their intrinsic values, he would receive about $5.00 Cdn. after closing the position.

It is easy to see that Mr. Fancy could never make *more* than $2.25 Cdn. on his spread. Indeed, no matter how high the stock went, he would still be forced to sell the stock at $40.00 Cdn. when February 40 calls were exercised! In other words, the difference between the intrinsic values of February 40 calls and February 35 calls cannot become larger than $5.00 Cdn.

Now we can build the Profit/Loss Profile of a vertical bullish call spread as in Figure 27. The same information can be presented in graph form as in Figure 28:

Stock Price	Profit or Loss
$ 1.00	$ −2.75
10.00	−2.75
30.00	−2.75
34.00	−2.75
35.00	−2.75
36.00	−1.75
37.00	−0.75
37.75	0.00
38.00	+0.25
39.00	+1.25
40.00	+2.25
41.00	+2.25
45.00	+2.25
50.00	+2.25
60.00	+2.25
80.00	+2.25
100.00	+2.25
200.00	+2.25

Figure 27   Figure 28

Figures 27 and 28 illustrate one of the reasons why I recommend avoiding spreads. You remember, of course, that in order for a strategy to work in the long run its Reward/Risk Ratio must be greater than 100%. Keeping that in mind, take another look at the Profit/Loss Profile of Mr. Fancy's spread. The best he can do is to make $2.25 Cdn. The worst that can happen is that he loses $2.75 Cdn. His Reward Risk Ratio is, therefore, equal to:

$$\frac{\$2.25}{\$2.75} \times 100\% = 82\%.$$

which is obviously less than 100%. This fact alone is sufficient for rejecting the strategy in this particular case.

Practically, most spreads have a Reward/Risk Ratio lower than 100%. Nevertheless, from time to time, one finds an exceptional spread with the Reward/Risk Ratio greater than 100%. Unfortunately, even such spreads are plagued with serious problems. The most important of these problems is that of timing.

When you buy calls or puts, you seldom intend to wait until expiration. On the contrary, you hope that the expected move in the underlying stock will happen soon and you will close the position at a profit. Indeed, when the underlying stock rallies strongly, calls respond by becoming more expensive. When the stock declines sharply, puts respond by going up in price. The call buyer and the put buyer take their profits as soon as the underlying stock has moved far enough in the "right" direction. They don't care if after the expected move the underlying stock returns to its initial level or even goes far in the opposite direction.

The position of a spread owner is much more difficult. Let us return for a moment to our friend Mr. Fancy. The spread he bought was undoubtedly bullish as illustrated by Figures 27 and 28. He was going to make money if Imperial Oil moved up, and he was going to incur a loss if the stock declined. However, the timing of the move was much more crucial than if Mr. Fancy simply bought calls instead of a spread. Indeed, in order to close the spread at a full profit of $2.25 Cdn., Mr. Fancy had to sell his February 35 calls for $5.00 Cdn. more than he had to pay for the February 40 calls in order to buy them back. The only time the prices of the two series of calls would differ by $5.00 Cdn. was when both calls were trading at their respective intrinsic values. That, in turn, would happen either when Imperial Oil rallied as high as $45.00 Cdn. or close to expiration.

To illustrate this point, imagine that the stock quickly ran up to $43.00 Cdn. and then fell back to $35.00 Cdn. and stayed there until expiration. When it reached $43.00 Cdn., the most probable price of February 35 calls was about $8.00 − $9.00 Cdn., while the most probable price of February 40 calls was $5.00 − $6.00 Cdn. The difference between the two prices was below $5.00 Cdn., which means that Mr. Fancy could not realize his maximum profit of $2.25 Cdn. He had a choice of either taking a much smaller profit (which would further hurt his Reward/Risk Ratio), or waiting in hope that Imperial Oil did not return to the $35.00 Cdn. level. When the stock declined and refused to rally again, Mr. Fancy ended up losing his entire investment of $2.75 Cdn. per share.

If instead of buying the spread, Mr. Fancy simply bought February 40 calls at their initial price of $2.50 Cdn., he could sell them at a more than 100% profit when Imperial Oil ran up to $43.00 Cdn. As you have seen, however, he could not close the spread at a sufficient profit at the same time.

This timing factor makes buying spreads even more difficult than buying calls or puts. In order to make money on a vertical spread, you must first find an exceptional one with the Reward/Risk Ratio higher than 100%. Then you must either expect a super-powerful rally in the underlying stock, or you must be able to predict that the stock will be above a particular level around the expiration time. It is hard enough to forecast a rally in the stock between now and expiration, but to forecast the level of the stock price *at* expiration is next to impossible!

This is exactly why I do not recommend spreads. If you are bullish on the stock, buy calls. If there are no calls that would satisfy all the appropriate Rules, check out the possibility of writing puts. If that fails as well, do not turn to spreads. Either buy the stock or, if you are determined to use options, look for another opportunity.

This entire discussion of problems associated with spreads might have left you wondering why they are so popular. In my opinion, the reason could be found in an optical illusion. In fact, this illusion is so strong and so attractive, that it has led to the creation of yet another option myth. The myth states that spreads are less risky than calls or puts. My answer to that is: nonsense!

In order to dispose of the myth, let us deal with the underlying optical illusion. Here is how it works.

If Mr. Fancy bought February 35 calls, he would have paid $5.25 Cdn. per share. When he bought these same calls as part of a spread, he paid only $2.75 Cdn. per share. Since, in both cases, he could lose his entire investment, it *appears* that buying the spread was safer since the risk was lower. This appearance, however, is misleading.

The correct statement is that all the money invested in calls and all the money invested in a spread are at risk. If you put $5,000.00 into calls, you can lose the entire $5,000.00. If you invest the same amount in a spread, your risk will be exactly the same: $5,000.00. Of course, since the spread is cheaper on a per share basis than the calls, you can buy more contracts in a spread using the same amount of funds than through calls. The larger number of contracts would seem to increase your leverage. However, this effect will be nullified by the fact that the maximum potential profit on a spread is limited, while that on calls is unlimited.

In short, calls are better than bullish spreads and puts are better than bearish spreads.

You can easily repeat the above analysis in relation to other vertical spreads. Their Profit/Loss Profiles are very similar; their Reward/Risk Ratios are usually below 100% and they all require unreasonable precision in the forecast of the time of the move in the underlying stock. In addition, vertical bullish put spread and vertical bearish call spread involve writing options that are already in-the-money. Such options can be exercised at any time, especially puts. If you try these spreads in practice, you will be annoyed repeatedly by having your short options exercised long before you are ready to close the spread.

Enough of vertical spreads. A calendar spread is quite a different animal. It consists of calls (or puts) with the same strike price but different expiration months. Calendar spreads are neither bullish, nor bearish. They are truly neutral. Let us have a close look at one of them.

On September 27, 1984, Inco was trading at $15.00 Cdn. on the Toronto Stock Exchange. On that day Miss Wizkid bought 10 Inco February 15 calls at $1.50 Cdn. and simultaneously wrote 10 Inco November 15 calls for $0.80 Cdn. In other words, she bought herself a calendar spread. What was she trying to achieve?

If Inco went up, both November 15 calls and February 15 calls would go up. The stronger the rally, the deeper both series would get in-the-money and the closer they would trade to their intrinsic values. However, their intrinsic values are always equal because they have the same strike price. As a result, the higher the price of Inco, the closer the prices of the two series of calls. If Miss Wizkid is finally forced to close the spread by buying back November 15 calls and selling February 15 calls at the same price, she will end up losing her entire investment in the spread equal to $1.50 − $0.80 = $0.70 Cdn. per share. Obviously, Miss Wizkid did not expect Inco to rally when she bought her spread.

If Inco declined, both series of calls would start losing value. If the stock declined quickly or if it declined slowly and did not recover by the expiration date, both series of calls would become completely worthless and expire as such. In this case Miss Wizkid would still lose her entire investment. Therefore, she was not enthusiastic about the prospect of Inco declining from its level of $15.00 Cdn.

The only other course of behaviour for Inco was to hover around $15.00 Cdn. This is exactly what Miss Wizkid was counting on. The longer Inco stayed around $15.00 Cdn., the faster would the premium disappear on the calls with the close expiry. In other words, November 15 calls would be losing value faster than February 15 calls. If November 15 calls declined to $0.10 Cdn., while February 15 calls declined to only $1.30 Cdn., Miss Wizkid could close her position by selling the February 15 calls and buying back the November 15 calls for a profit of $0.80 − $1.50 + $1.30 − $0.10 = $0.50 Cdn. Since her entire investment was equal to $0.70 Cdn., the return on it would be quite good. At least it would look that way until commissions took their mighty bite out of the profit.

The sum up, Miss Wizkid was using a legitimate strategy for capitalizing on reduced volatility. But haven't we seen another strategy applicable under the same circumstances? Indeed we have. In Chapter 7, we analyzed writing straddles and combinations as a means of capitalizing on decreased volatility.

On the same day, September 27, 1984, Miss Wizkid could write a straddle on Inco by writing November 15 calls for $0.80 Cdn. and writing November 15 puts for $0.50 Cdn. Let us compare this position with her calendar spread.

The highest profit on the calendar spread could theoretically be $0.80 Cdn. In order for that profit to be realized, November 15 calls had to decline to $0.00 Cdn., while February 15 calls had to retain their full value of $1.50 Cdn., which is quite impossible in practice.

The maximum profit of the straddle could be equal to $0.80 + $0.50 = $1.30 Cdn. This profit would be realized if Inco expired at $15.00 Cdn. The closer the stock was trading to this magic number at expiration, the closer would the profit come to $1.30 Cdn. Therefore, the profit potential of the position would be much higher in the case of a straddle.

As long as Inco remained between $16.30 Cdn. and $13.70 Cdn., the straddle remained profitable (at least before commissions). At the same time, a quick move to either $16.30 Cdn. or $13.70 Cdn. would have destroyed the potential profitability of the calendar spread, because after such a move the two option series involved in the spread would be trading very close to each other.

My experience shows that short straddles and combinations are far superior to calendar spreads when the investor expects a reduction in the volatility of the underlying stock.

The last comment about spreads deals with closing them in stages. Many spread players try to squeeze more out of a spread by closing one side and leaving the other open. I do not like it a single bit! Such behaviour stems from a change in the game plan and we have already discussed its dangers. Even though one might get lucky and make a higher profit by closing the two sides of a spread at different times, if he keeps doing that he will develop the habit of changing the strategy in the middle of the game. This is equivalent to a total loss of discipline, and the lack of discipline is fatal for an investor. Never change your plan in the middle of the game!

And once again: Do not use spreads!

Chapter 10

Cash Management

Chapters 5 to 9 of this book were devoted to analyses of various option strategies. In strategy analysis, we were most interested in the bottom line and the Reward/Risk Ratio. Consequently, we performed all calculations on a per share basis paying little attention to the overall amounts of money involved in each transaction.

This chapter deals with all those total amounts of money that have been disregarded so far. Once you have decided to use a particular strategy, be it buying calls or writing combinations, you have to know how much money you can invest in the transaction. No calculation performed on a per share basis will help you to find the answer.

It is amazing that most option literature never even mentions the problem of cash management. Examples presented in this chapter will illustrate that cash management is at least as important as the proper selection of a strategy. Yet numerous volumes have been written on strategies and very few words about managing one's total funds in relation to each option transaction.

As a matter of fact, cash management is so important that some Rules related to it had to be injected in previous chapters. One was setting the limitation on how many contracts you can afford to buy:

Rule 1: NEVER PUT MORE MONEY INTO BUYING OPTIONS THAN YOU ARE PREPARED TO LOSE.

The second Rule dealt with the same question in relation to writing options. As you remember, the risk of an option writer is often unlimited or very large. In order to create a Reward/Risk Ratio greater than 100%, I recommended using mental stop-losses. The measuring stick for the distance from a strike price to the stop-loss has always been the amount of money received at the time of writing. Consequently, the same amount was used to measure the risk of the position. Once you know the risk of a position, you can figure out the maximum number of contracts you can afford:

Rule 16: WHEN WRITING UNCOVERED OPTIONS, THE AMOUNT OF MONEY YOU RECEIVE SHOULD NOT EXCEED THE AMOUNT OF MONEY YOU ARE PREPARED TO LOSE.

Rules 1 and 16 are very good for preventing disastrously large losses on any given trade. These Rules, as all the others dicussed in this chapter, do not apply to stock-related strategies. In those strategies, the number of option contracts involved is determined by the number of shares of the underlying stock which is being held or is intended to be held. The Rules for cash management are applicable only to "pure" option strategies in which position in the underlying stock is not involved. The importance of cash management for "pure" option strategies is illustrated by the following example:

Imagine an investor who believed that he could catch short-term fluctuations in the price of Sears Roebuck. On April 13, 1984, the stock was trading at $30.75 US and our investor expected a short-term rally. Accordingly, he bought September 30 calls at $3.00 US per share.

The rally came as expected and in exactly two weeks, on April 27, 1984, Sears was quoted at $33.75 US. Our investor sold his calls for $4.75 US.

By May 4, 1984, Sears Roebuck declined to $32.13 US and, according to the analysis of the investor, was ready to rally again. The investor bought September 35 calls at $1.50 US.

This time something went wrong and the stock refused to reach the higher levels forecasted by the investor. On June 15, 1984, he gave up and sold the calls for $0.50 US, while the stock was trading at $30.00 US.

The investor did not give up. Having been born under the sign of Taurus, he was known among his friends for outstanding persistence. As soon as Sears Roebuck showed signs of strengthening, the investor was back in the game. On July 27, 1984, with the stock trading at $32.50 US, he bought September 30 calls at $3.00 US.

As often before, the investor's persistence was rewarded. By August 3, 1984, Sears Roebuck had climbed up to $34.75 US, and the investor sold his calls for $5.00 US.

Here is the question: After this series of three trades, how did the investor do? Did he make a profit, and if yes, then how much?

Amazingly enough, we do not have an answer to this simple and natural question.

Looking at it one way, the investor had two gains and only one loss. This sounds like a good result. Who would refuse having twice as many victories as defeats?

Looking at it differently, the total profit per share was equal to $4.75 − $3.00 + $0.50 − $1.50 + $5.00 − $3.00 = $2.75 US. It is definitely a profit, but somehow it does not look as impressive as two gains to one loss.

Calculating the results on a percentage basis would show that the investor made 58% on the first trade, lost 67% on the second one and made 67% on the third. It is completely unclear what to do with these percentages in order to assess the result of trading.

The truth is that we do not have enough information to answer the question of how well the investor did. What we have to know is how much money he put into every trade. Then we wouldn't have to guess or get involved in complicated mathematical discussions of percentages and other abstract phenomena. If we knew how much money the investor put into every trade, or how many contracts he bought every time, we could calculate his profit or loss to a penny.

Let us expand this example and imagine that instead of one, there were three different investors, who performed the above described series of trades of Sears Roebuck options. We will further assume that all three started with the same amount of money, but employed different money management strategies.

The first one, Mr. Gambler, started with $30,000.00 US. Being true to his name, he threw the entire amount into the first trade. On April 13, 1984, he bought 100 Sears Roebuck September 30 calls at $3.00 US. (In this example we ignore commissions which are not important for the point in question.) On April 27, 1984, he sold these calls for $4.75 US. His total capital was now equal to $47,500.00 US.

On May 4, 1984, Mr. Gambler re-invested his entire capital by buying 316 Sears Roebuck September 32 calls at $1.50 US. When he sold the calls at $0.50 US on June 15, 1984, all that was left of his capital was $15,900.00 US. Needless to say, Mr. Gambler was not very happy.

On July 27, 1984, he moved in again, buying 53 Sears Roebuck September 30 calls at $3.00 US. He wanted to buy more, but that was all he could afford on the remnants of his capital. As we know, the trade turned out well, and Mr. Gambler sold the calls for $5.00 US on August 3, 1984. He received the total of $26,500.00 US for the calls.

Mr. Gambler had nothing to celebrate. Despite the fact that he had two gains and only one loss, despite the per-share and percentage calculations, which all turned out in his favour, he still lost $3,500.00 US.

The second investor, Mr. Consistent, also started with $30,000.00 US, but he was far too cautious to throw it all into one trade. Instead, he put $25,500.00 US in the bank as a reserve and used $4,500.00 US to buy 15 Sears Roebuck September 30 calls at $3.00 US on April 13, 1984. When he sold the calls for $4.75 US on April 27, 1984, his total capital had grown to $32,625.00 US. (We are ignoring not only commissions, but interest also.)

Before entering the next transaction, Mr. Consistent performed the following calculation. Since he started with $4,500.00 US out of the total capital of $30,000.00 US, his initial investment was equal to 15% of the total capital. The new capital was equal to $32,625.00 US, and Mr. Consistent was prepared to risk 15% of it in the next trade. On May 4, 1984, he bought 32 Sears Roebuck September 35 calls at $1.50 US. The total amount of the purchase was $4,800.00 US. As you remember, the trade turned sour, and the sale price of the calls was $0.50 US on June 15, 1984. The total capital of Mr. Consistent shrank to $29,425.00 US.

Fifteen per cent of the new total amount was equal to $4,413.75 US. This was how much Mr. Consistent was prepared to invest in the third trade. Consequently, on July 27, 1984, he bought 14 Sears Roebuck September 30 calls at $3.00 US. When he sold these calls for $5.00 US on August 3, 1984, he received $7,000.00 US. Adding this amount to his reserve, he calculated his total capital to be equal to $32,225.00 US.

Mr. Consistent was rather pleased with himself. In less than four months he had made a $2,225.00 US profit on the original investment of $30,000.00 US.

The third investor, Mr. Safe, began with the same amount of $30,000.00 US. His first step was identical with that of Mr. Consistent. He put $25,500.00 US in the bank and used the rest to buy 15 Sears Roebuck September 30 calls at $3.00 US on April 13, 1984. He sold the calls for $4.75 US on April 27, 1984, and saw his total capital grow to $32,625.00 US.

This is where the routes of Mr. Safe and Mr. Consistent parted. Instead of re-investing 15% of his new total capital, Mr. Safe put the entire profit of $2,625.00 US in the bank and reinvested only the initial $4,500.00 US by buying 30 Sears Roebuck September 35 calls at $1.50 US on May 4, 1984. On June 15, 1984, Mr. Safe sold the calls for $0.50 US and lost $3,000.00 US. His total capital was now equal to $29,625.00 US.

In order to stay in the game, Mr. Safe was forced to dip into his reserve. On July 27, 1984, he withdrew $3,000.00 US from his bank account and invested the unchanged initial amount of $4,500.00 US in 15 Sears Roebuck September 30 calls at $3.00 US. When he sold the calls for $5.00 US on August 3, 1984, his total capital grew to $32,625.00 US.

The net profit of Mr. Safe was equal to $2,625.00 US, which was higher than the profit of Mr. Consistent.

As this example shows, the same series of trades can produce very different results, from good to terrible, depending on the cash management strategy.

A cash management strategy is a series of rules that dictate how much money you should invest in each trade and what you should do with profits and losses. The strategy used by Mr. Gambler in our example, is called "pyramiding." Unfortunately, it is a very popular strategy with option buyers. I say "unfortunately," because this cash management strategy guarantees that the investor using it will eventually lose all his money. What is amazing is that the outcome does not depend on how good such an investor is at forecasting stocks and selecting the best options. Pyramiding guarantees a total loss!

Indeed, the strategy of pyramiding consists of re-investing the entire amount of capital in the next trade. No matter how good one's forecasting ability is, sooner or later he will be dead wrong. Since his entire capital will be invested in one position at that time, he will lose it all! It turns out that Mr. Gambler was quite lucky to get some of his money back!

There are several modifications of pyramiding, but they all lead to the same result. For example, some investors use only a portion of their total capital in the first trade, but after that re-invest all profits. As a result, sooner or later they lose the portion invested in the first trade, and are forced to dip into the reserve. If they continue re-investing all profits, eventually they lose the entire capital.

Some investors try to re-invest only the first few profits, after which they are ready to switch to a more conservative cash management strategy. The flaw in their logic lies in the assumption that the first few trades are going to be profitable. They are not prepared for a series of mistakes right at the beginning of trading.

And yet this is the first question that a prudent investor must tackle. If you start with a series of losses, how much capital can you afford to put into every position in order to be able to continue investing despite the losses? This most important question is asked all too rarely. Most of the big losers in options are those who invested too much money in a few, or even one, unfortunate positions, sustained large losses and could not continue. They forgot that the first priority of any investor should be the preservation of capital.

In order to calculate the percentage of capital you can put in one position, we must make some assumptions about your forecasting ability. Let us assume that you are right about the behaviour of the underlying stock 65% of the time. If your batting average is much worse than that, you should forget about options and do more work on stocks. In order to make money in the long run, you must be right about 65% of the time.

Assuming that your average rate of success is 65%, we can apply the Probability Theory in order to calculate the odds of any series of losses. For example, the probability of six losses in a row would be less than two out of a thousand. This probability is low enough to suggest that if your capital is sufficient for six tries in a row, you are in good shape. In other words, you should not invest more than one sixth of the capital you have set aside for options in any one position.

Rule 42: YOUR INITIAL INVESTMENT IN OPTIONS, MEASURED BY THE AMOUNT YOU ARE PREPARED TO LOSE, SHOULD NOT EXCEED 15% OF THE TOTAL CAPITAL AVAILABLE FOR OPTIONS.

This Rule applies to both buying and writing of uncovered options. If you are a buyer, your risk is measured by the amount of money you pay for the options. Therefore, you should not pay out more than 15% of the total option capital for one long position. If you are a writer, your risk is measured by the amount of money you receive (through mental stop-losses). Therefore, the amount of money you receive should not exceed 15% of the total option capital.

I would like to note that one should be extremely careful when trying to by-pass Rule 42 through diversification. For example, if you buy calls on two different stocks at the same time, you should not invest 15% of your total option capital in each position. If you do that, you will have 30% of your capital invested on the same side of the market. A sharp decline in the market as a whole would ruin both positions at the same time.

On the other hand, if you own a straddle on one stock and you have 15% of the capital invested in that straddle, you can still buy calls or puts on another stock and invest another 15% of the capital. In this situation, a sharp move of the market one way or another will not ruin both positions at the same time.

Similarly, you can put 15% of your capital into long calls on one stock and another 15% into long puts on another stock. Such a combined position cannot be destroyed by one unfavourable move of the market.

Once your first trade is completed, you will have either a loss or a gain. Either way your total capital will have changed. How much should you invest in the next trade? I recommend the strategy used by Mr. Safe in the example presented earlier in this chapter. Keep the number of dollars you invest in every position constant, irrespective of gains and losses. By doing this you will quickly discover if your total capital is growing or declining. If it is declining, you should stop and check for problems with stock forecasting and option strategies. If the capital is growing you should wait until it doubles before you change anything.

Rule 43: YOU SHOULD INVEST THE SAME NUMBER OF DOLLARS (MEASURED BY THE AMOUNT YOU ARE PREPARED TO LOSE) IN BUYING OR WRITING UNCOVERED OPTIONS UNTIL YOU HAVE DOUBLED YOUR TOTAL CAPITAL AVAILABLE FOR OPTIONS.

So you have doubled the capital and you feel intelligent, happy, and very confident. What next? In my opinion, this is the best time to get ready for a cold shower. It is exactly when one feels omnipotent that one makes the most stupid mistakes. Knowing this, I prefer giving myself a cold shower rather than relying on bad luck and judgment to provide one for me. Here is what I do and what I recommend to you:

Rule 44: WHEN YOU HAVE DOUBLED THE TOTAL CAPITAL AVAILABLE FOR OPTIONS FOR THE FIRST TIME, YOU SHOULD REMOVE HALF OF IT AND WITHDRAW IT FROM INVESTING IN OPTIONS.

In other words, you remove the initial capital. If you started with $30,000 and doubled it through investing in options, you should remove the initial $30,000. After that you will be investing your profits only. Even if you lose the entire $30,000, you would break even overall, since your initial capital will be safe and intact. This knowledge that you can break even at the worst will remove all anxiety and drastically improve your decision-making ability.

Unfortunately, if you continue to remove half of the capital every time you double the money, you won't get very far. Ultimately, you would like to see the employed capital and the profits grow accordingly. Therefore, when you double your capital for the second time, instead of withdrawing half of it, you should double the stakes. By this time, your stock forecasting ability and the selection of option strategies will have withstood the test of time. After that you will keep doubling the stakes every time you have doubled the capital:

Rule 45: WHEN YOU HAVE DOUBLED THE TOTAL CAPITAL AVAILABLE FOR OPTIONS FOR THE SECOND, THIRD, ETC., TIME, YOU SHOULD DOUBLE THE AMOUNT OF MONEY YOU ARE PREPARED TO LOSE.

Now you have the entire cash management strategy before you. First you decide how much money you are setting aside for options. Then you start investing 15% of it at a time. Once you have doubled the total amount, you withdraw a half. After that, every time you have doubled the capital, you double the stakes. This is the road to riches!

Chapter 11

Conversions and Equivalences

When we analyzed various strategies in the previous chapters of the book, we discovered that some strategies were equivalent to others. For example, simultaneous covered writing is equivalent to writing uncovered puts, while buying calls is equivalent to buying the underlying stock and buying puts against it. The reason for the existence of these equivalences is a mathematical relationship between the prices of a stock, its calls, puts, interest rates, and dividends. In this chapter, we will examine this relationship and some of its important applications.

Let us start with an example. Imagine that on September 27, 1984, you bought 100 shares of Imasco at $42.00 Cdn., wrote one Imasco January 40 call for $3.50 Cdn. and bought one Imasco January 40 put at $0.60 Cdn. What was the Profit/Loss Profile of your position?

If Imasco declined to $40.00 Cdn. and remained at that price until expiration, both January 40 calls and January 40 puts would expire worthless. In order to close the position you would have to sell your 100 shares for $40.00 Cdn. Your net profit would be equal to $40.00 − $42.00 + $3.50 − $0.60 = $0.90 Cdn.

If Imasco remained above $40.00 Cdn. until expiration, your short January 40 call would eventually be exercised, which would force you to sell your shares for the strike price of $40.00 Cdn. Of course, the January 40 put would expire worthless. Since you would have been forced to sell the stock at $40.00 Cdn., your net profit would be equal to the same $0.90 Cdn.

If Imasco declined below $40.00 Cdn. and stayed there until expiration, January 40 calls would expire worthless. You would then have a choice of selling your shares in the market for the market price (which would be below $40.00 Cdn.) or to exercise your January 40 put and sell the shares at the strike price of $40.00 Cdn. You would certainly prefer to exercise the put. As a result, your net profit would be equal to the same $0.90 Cdn.

As you can see, no matter what happens with the underlying stock, the position described above would yield the same profit of $0.90 Cdn. per share. In other words, this profit is indeed "locked-in."

The prices in this example, as in all other examples in this book, are the ones that actually existed on that day. Therefore, professional option traders, who do not pay commissions, could actually take this position and lock in a profit of $0.90 Cdn. without any risk. Why were they not doing it?

The reason is that the profit of $0.90 Cdn. would be just enough to cover the cost of money. In order to take a position like this one, an investor would have to pay for the stock and for the put. His payment would be reduced by the amount he received for the call. This amount of money is then tied in the position and would not earn interest. On the other hand, the investor would be receiving dividends paid on the stock. The difference between the interest that the investor was foregoing by entering this position and the dividends he was going to receive was equal to exactly $0.90 Cdn. per share. In other words, the prices of the stock, the calls, the puts, the rate of dividends, and the rate of interest available on free cash were in perfect balance. This balance can be described by the following mathematical equation:

$$\text{STOCK PRICE} + \text{PUT PRICE} + \text{INTEREST} =$$
$$\text{CALL PRICE} + \text{STRIKE PRICE} + \text{DIVIDENDS}$$

This formula is called the *Conversion Formula* and the position consisting of long stock, long puts, and short calls is called *a conversion*. The reason for such a name will become obvious a little later.

The Conversion Formula describes the condition of balance between its elements. Such balance is often disturbed by buying and selling pressures in the market. For example, if all other elements remain constant except for the price of the calls which goes up due to demand, the equilibrium will be disturbed. Returning to our example, if the calls became $0.50 Cdn. more expensive while all other prices and rates remained the same, the described conversion position would become profitable. It would allow the investor to lock in a profit of $0.90 + $0.50 = $1.40 Cdn. per share, which was $0.50 Cdn. more than the cost of money minus the dividends. As a result, professional traders would start accumulating this position. Their activity would depress the prices of the calls (because they would be writing those calls) and/or raise the prices of the stock and the puts until the equilibrium was re-established.

If the price of the calls declined instead of rising, while all the other elements remained the same, the opposite position would become profitable. Professional traders would start shorting the stock, writing puts and buying calls, until the equilibrium was once more re-established. The position opposite to a conversion is called *a reversed conversion* or *a reconversion*. Both conversions and reconversions are sometimes called *tripods*.

The only people who can and do make money on conversions and reconversions are professional traders. Since they do not pay commissions, they move in if they can make a profit of $0.50 or even $0.25 per share. Their buying and selling restores the balance expressed by the Conversion Formula long before the discrepancy becomes so great that other investors, who pay commissions, can move in and make a profit. Consequently, conversions and reconversions cannot be used by anyone except professional option traders. However, understanding these positions is necessary for all option traders and also for many stock market analysts who do not deal in options.

The first important fact to be learned from the Conversion Formula is that many option strategies are equivalent to one another. I am going to list several versions of the Formula, which are all equivalent to one another. Even though all these versions express exactly the same relationship, each one of them illustrates one particular relationship between various strategies. Here are the formulae:

1. STOCK PRICE + PUT PRICE = CALL PRICE + STRIKE PRICE + DIVIDENDS − INTEREST.
2. PUT PRICE = CALL PRICE − STOCK PRICE + STRIKE PRICE + DIVIDENDS − INTEREST.
3. STOCK PRICE − CALL PRICE = − PUT PRICE + STRIKE PRICE + DIVIDENDS − INTEREST.
4. CALL PRICE = STOCK PRICE + PUT PRICE − STRIKE PRICE − DIVIDENDS + INTEREST.
5. STOCK PRICE = CALL PRICE − PUT PRICE + STRIKE PRICE + DIVIDENDS − INTEREST.

The first formula expresses the relationship which we discovered empirically in Chapter 8, i.e. that buying a stock and buying puts against it (in other words, buying protective puts) is equivalent to buying calls.

The second formula shows that buying puts is equivalent to buying calls and selling the underlying stock short. This equivalence explains the term "Conversion Formula." Historically, call options appeared long before put options. Investors who used call options when they were bullish on the underlying stock, wanted to have a similar instrument for playing the downside swings as well. Since there were no put options, they invented the technique of shorting the stock and buying calls against the short position. As formula 2 shows, the resulting position is equivalent to a long put. As a result, the position consisting of short stock and long calls is called *a synthetic put.*

The left side of the third formula consists of long stock and short calls, which is the famous covered writing position. The right side contains puts with the sign minus, i.e. short puts. As we discovered in Chapters 8 and 9, covered writing is indeed equivalent to writing uncovered puts. This equivalence destroys the popular myth that covered writing is a very conservative and safe strategy while writing uncovered options is pure gambling. The formula shows that the two are simply equivalent!

The fourth formula illustrates the fact that buying calls is equivalent to buying the stock and buying puts. As a result, the position consisting of long stock and long puts is called *a synthetic call.*

The fifth formula shows that buying a stock is equivalent to buying its calls and writing the corresponding puts. Therefore, the position consisting of long calls and short puts is called *a synthetic stock.*

The benefit of understanding these relationships is in the drastic reduction of the number of possible option strategies. Whenever you are confronted with a complex combination of stock, calls and puts, the Conversion Formula will help you to break it down to a few familiar elements. This will simplify analysis and save you a lot of time.

In addition to the equivalences between many option strategies, the Conversion Formula illustrates the futility of searching for significant market anomalies in the prices of options. These anomalies existed during the period when computers were too slow to go through all the possible triple combinations of stocks, calls, and puts in a matter of seconds. Without the aid of computers, even very experienced traders could notice some of the discrepancies only by chance. When they found one, they immediately started accumulating a conversion or a reconversion until the anomaly was liquidated.

With the development of faster computers, professional option traders have acquired the ability to screen all possible triple combinations every few minutes and to jump into the ones that are out of balance. As a result, the anomalies have practically disappeared. At present, the prices of calls, puts, and the underlying stocks are very close to a perfect balance at all times. Consequently, looking for anomalies has become a waste of time. The only way to make money in options now is to be equally good at forecasting stocks and selecting proper option strategies with relation to the stock forecast.

While conversions and reconversions have eliminated some opportunities by bringing the prices in balance, they have also created an opportunity where there had been none. Imagine a stock that is generally considered to be bullish. Due to high demand, its calls are usually also very expensive in relation to the stock price. In many cases, their prices are so high that an investor cannot buy them without violating one of the Rules for buying calls.

Before the computerization of conversions, the puts on such a stock were usually very cheap. If most investors believe that the stock is going higher, there isn't much demand for the puts. Consequently, not only were the calls too expensive to buy, but puts were too cheap to write. In other words, it was impossible to use options as a reasonable vehicle.

As the use of conversions grew, the situation started changing. If you return to formula 2 and freeze all the elements except for the calls and the puts, you will find out that if calls go up, puts also have to go up! The more expensive the calls become, relative to the underlying stock, the more expensive are the puts. Therefore, if the calls are too expensive to buy, the puts are most probably not too cheap to write!

A similar opportunity exists in the case of a bearish stock. If the majority of option players consider the stock bearish, its puts might be far too expensive for buying. The same formula 2 suggests that as the price of the puts expands relative to the underlying stock, so does the price of the calls. Consequently, if the puts are too expensive for buying, the calls are also expensive and could very well be suitable for writing.

In this way conversions have replaced one opportunity with another.

Another area to which conversions brought some major changes is related to some popular indicators for market trends and timing. One such tool is the volume of trading in a stock. In the absence of options, unusually high volume indicated unusually active trading. Various techniques have been developed in order to determine if the pressure is coming from the buyers or from the sellers. The correct assessment of the direction of the unusually strong pressure can help to forecast the direction of the next move.

With the growing popularity of options, the usefulness of this technique diminished. On one hand, active buying of calls instead of the stock itself, does not distort the picture. Even though the public buys the calls rather than the stock, the floor traders and specialists, who are selling all these calls to the public, do not enjoy accumulating a large short position in the calls on a bullish stock. They hedge their position by buying the same stock. As a result, the volume of buying calls by the public is translated into the volume of buying the stock by the specialists. In this particular case, there is no distortion of the stock volume to option trading.

On the other hand, when large option positions are exercised, the numbers of shares purchased or sold through exercise become a part of the trading volume. Since purchases and sales of stock through exercise happen at a predetermined price, they do not result in bullish or bearish pressures on the stock. Since most options are exercised around the expiry dates, this results in splashes of high volume whose timing is determined by the calendar of exercises rather than by the changes in the mood of investors. Such occurrences of high volume have no value for stock forecasting. In fact, they are downright misleading. But there is no way of separating such volume from the "genuine" trading volume.

Conversions add to the confusion. When a minor anomaly arises in the prices of options, due to the imbalance of supply and demand from the public, floor traders and specialists rush in to lock some profits in conversions or reconversions. Since establishing such positions involves buying or selling the underlying stock, the volume associated with conversions and reconversions shows together with the volume of other trading. A trader buying or selling a conversion, however, is neither bullish nor bearish on the underlying stock. He is simply using a divergence in order to lock in a profit. Consequently, the volume generated by the activity in conversions and reconversions is also misleading.

Another popular trend indicator is the short interest. The short interest is the total number of shares sold short in a given stock or in the market as a whole. Before conversions and reconversions became very popular, high short interest served as a good bullish indicator. The reason is very simple. When the stock is moving up, all the owners of short positions get margin calls with requests for additional funds. The majority of short sellers do not add to the initial margin. Instead, they agree to have their position covered at the market. Since covering a short position in the stock means buying this stock, short positions supply additional fuel for rallies. The stronger the rally, the more margin calls, the more covering at the market, the more buying, the stronger the rally, etc. As you can see, "genuine" short interest creates a snowball effect during a strong rally. This is why it used to be such a good bullish indicator.

Today, the total numbers for short interest include the short positions locked in reverse conversions. These positions cannot provide fuel for any rally because they are not subject to margin calls. Profits in these positions are locked in. Moreover, when reverse conversions are covered, it is done by exercising the options involved rather than by buying the stock in the market. Therefore, even closing such positions does not have any bullish or bearish implications. Since we cannot separates the "genuine" short interest from the short positions locked in reconversions, the usefulness of this indicator has been reduced to zero.

As you can see, even though you might never do a conversion or a reconversion yourself, understanding them can be very helpful in your investment strategies and analyses.

Chapter 12

Options On Other Instruments

The success of options on stocks (or equity options) in the seventies resulted in the flood of new options in the eighties. Within the first four years of the decade, investors witnessed the birth of options on bonds, options on financial futures, options on currencies, options on precious metals, options on agricultural commodities, options on stock market indices and subindices, options on future contracts on stock market indices, etc. Various Exchanges keep listing new options because the Exchanges make their profits on the volume of trading. As far as the investors are concerned, new options give them a chance to try new strategies for making profits in their favourite financial instruments.

Only time will tell which of these options will become popular enough to survive. Many of them will undouubtedly disappear due to the lack of interest. Some are dying already.

Fortunately, the differences between various underlying financial instruments have very little effect on option strategies. For example, call options always rise in price when the underlying security rallies; puts go up when the underlying security takes a nosedive; spreads limit both risk and profit; straddles and combinations offer a play on the change in volatility.

We do not have to repeat the analysis performed in the earlier chapters of this book for every new financial instrument on which options are being traded. In fact, most of the Rules in Chapter 2 would need only minor modifications in order to become applicable to a different financial instrument. I think it is an excellent exercise for an investor to examine all the Rules as they would apply to options on the financial instruments other than stocks. The rationale for the Rules would remain the same. The investor's goal is to construct a strategy with a Reward/Risk Ratio greater than 100% and to apply this strategy within the confines of a sound cash management system. If this is done, the investor's success will depend only on his ability to forecast the behaviour of the underlying financial instrument.

Since the subject of this book is option strategies and cash management, it applies equally to all options. The principles and the analytical methods presented in this book are universal. Only minor details might differ from one financial instrument to the next.

One peculiarity of index options deserves special attention. The underlying instrument for index options is a stock market index or subindex which can be calculated but cannot be bought, sold, or physically delivered. This results in a different procedure for exercising index options. When such options are exercised, the buyer receives and the writer delivers the amount of cash equal to the intrinsic value of the option.

For example, if you bought a January 150 call option on the S&P 100 and if you decide to exercise it when the S&P 100 is trading at 162, you would receive $162 - 150 = 12$ times the number of units in one contract.

Since it is impossible to buy or sell a market index, conversions and reconversions cannot be based on index options. As a result, the relationships between the prices of calls, puts, indices, and interest rates, which were presented in the previous chapter, cannot be expected to be true for index options.

As far as the use of index options is concerned, they offer an opportunity to make money on forecasting the behaviour of the market as a whole rather than that of individual stocks. It is up to each investor to consider the use of these options in relation to his strengths and weaknesses. For example, if your forte is fundamental analysis, you will definitely be better in forecasting individual stocks than the market as a whole. On the other hand, if you are particularly good at market timing, it is easier for you to determine the trend of a broad market index rather than that of an individual stock.

Index options can also be used to protect a diversified portfolio of stocks against a general market decline. Buying index puts against such a portfolio is much cheaper than buying protective puts against individual stocks. In addition to that, not all stocks in your portfolio might be optionable.

Another interesting strategy involving index options is based on keeping 85% to 95% of your total capital in short-term interest bearing instruments and using the remainder of the funds to buy calls or puts on a broad market index. If you are a good market timer, such a strategy will produce excellent results during the periods when short-term interest rates are relatively high. In the environment of low interest rates this strategy will prove inferior to the one of investing 100% of your funds in the stocks on the long or short side.

With the variety of options and option strategies, the possibilities open to an investor are limited only by the investor's imagination and creativity. However, no matter what financial instrument the options are based on, the basic principles laid down in this book still apply. You must always analyze the Profit/Loss Profile of the strategy; you must always maintain a Reward/Risk Ratio greater than 100%; and you must always follow a rational cash management strategy similar to the one developed in Chapter 10. Last but definitely not least, you must have a good understanding of the underlying financial instrument in order to have a forecast with reliability of about 65%.

Once all the ingredients are in place, there will be nothing standing between you and your steadily growing profits!

Chapter 13

Conclusion

In the pages of this book, we have done step-by-step analyses of the most popular option strategies. The analyses were based on real-life examples of equity options, but the methods and the conclusions remain valid for options on any financial instruments.

The emphasis of this book is on practical tools for making money. Consequently, you have encountered few mathematical formulae and many practical Rules. These Rules cannot guarantee that all your trades will be profitable, but they will certainly help in loading the dice in your favour.

Following rules takes discipline. The absolute majority of big losses in the stock market (both in options and in other financial vehicles) result from the lack of discipline. I strongly recommend that you devote at least as much time and effort to the development of discipline as to the analysis of the market. Without discipline, even the best strategy based on the best forecasts, leads to financial disaster. That is why the history of the stock market is generously peppered with suicides. Discipline does not prevent mistakes, but it safeguards from gigantic losses. If you have difficulty developing discipline, you might consider taking an introductory course in yoga and practising just one element — full relaxation. Not only does it help to manage stress, but it also builds internal discipline.

I also suggest that you strike the work 'LUCK' out of your financial vocabulary. Not that luck does not exist; on the contrary, it most certainly does. However, if you invest actively over a long period of time, your good luck and bad luck will average out. Your net results will be the reflection of your skill alone. As strange as it seems, good luck in the stock market is actually very dangerous. Nothing pushes you harder toward breaking all rules and abandoning all discipline than a streak of good luck. When you are hitting one winner after another, you start feeling that you simply cannot go wrong. Once you have caught this suicidal idea crossing your mind, you should immediately withdraw some profits, re-read all the Rules, and remind yourself to stay humble. You will be very glad you have done all that when your luck changes!

If you enjoy options, you will find and create many strategies other than those presented in this book. Yet, they too, can be analyzed using the methods illustrated in previous chapters. Once you are comfortable with the new strategy, do not forget to subject it to the Rules of cash management. These Rules are universal. Disregard for them is usually punished by a quick shrinking of your bank account.

I have shared with you my knowledge and experience. All that is left is to wish you a lot of profits and as much fun!

And — of course — good luck!

Glossary

AT-THE-MONEY A call or put option is said to be at-the-money when the underlying stock is trading at the strike price of the option.

BEARISH FORECAST A forecast that calls for the financial instrument under consideration to decline in price is called bearish.

BULLISH FORECAST A forecast that calls for the financial instrument under consideration to increase in price is called bullish.

BUYING BACK A transaction which consists of buying a financial instrument in the market in order to cover a short position in this financial instrument is called buying it back.

BUYING A CALL When an investor buys the right to purchase a financial instrument at a fixed price during a fixed period of time, he is said to have bought a call option (or simply a call) on that financial instrument.

BUYING A PUT When an investor buys the right to sell a financial instrument at a fixed price during a fixed period of time, he is said to have bought a put option (or simply a put) on that financial instrument.

CALENDAR SPREAD A position consisting of an equal number of calls (or puts) on the same financial instrument with the same strike price and different expiration dates is called a calendar or a horizontal spread.

CALL OPTION   A contract that enables an investor to buy a certain financial instrument at a fixed price during a fixed period of time from another investor is called a call option (or simply a call) on that financial instrument.

COMBINATION   A position consisting of an equal number of calls and puts on the same financial instrument with the same expiration date but different strike prices is called a combination.

CONVERSION   A position consisting of a long underlying financial instrument and an equal number of short calls and long puts on that instrument with the same strike price and the same expiration date is called a conversion.

COVERED WRITING   A position consisting of a long underlying financial instrument and short calls on that instrument is called a covered writing position.

EXERCISING AN OPTION   Exercising the right to buy the underlying financial instrument (in the case of a call option) or sell it (in the case of a put option) by the owner of the option is called exercising the option.

EXERCISE PRICE   A predetermined price at which the owner of an option contract can buy (in the case of a call option) or sell (in the case of a put option) the underlying financial instrument is called an exercise price or a strike price.

EXPIRY DATE   The last day when the owner of an option contract can exercise his right to buy or sell the underlying financial instrument is called the expiration date or the expiry date.

FUTURE CONTRACT   An obligation to buy or sell the underlying financial insrument or commodity at a fixed price at a fixed date is called a future contract on that financial instrument or commodity.

IN-THE-MONEY   An option is said to be in-the-money if exercising it and immediately closing the resulting position in the underlying financial instrument at the market would yield a profit. In other words, an option is in-the-money if its intrinsic value is greater than zero.

INTRINSIC VALUE   The profit that can be realized on the underlying financial instrument by exercising the option and immediately closing the resulting position in that instrument is called the intrinsic value of that option.

LONG CALL   A position resulting from buying a call option is called a long call.

LONG COMBINATION   A position resulting from buying an equal number of calls and puts on the same financial instrument with the same expiration date but different strike prices is called a long combination.

LONG PUT   A position resulting from buying a put option is called a long put.

LONG STOCK   A position resulting from buying a stock is called a long stock.

LONG STRADDLE   A position resulting from buying an equal number of calls and puts on the same financial instrument with the same expiration date and the same strike price is called a long straddle.

MARGIN   The amount deposited with the investor's broker in order to cover possible losses in the investor's account is called a margin.

MENTAL STOP-LOSS   The price of the underlying financial instrument is called a mental stop-loss if the investor is going to close his position in that instrument and/or in options based on that instrument as soon as this price is reached. No order is placed with the broker in advance for the execution of a mental stop-loss.

NON-SIMULTANEOUS COVERED WRITING   The strategy consisting of writing calls against an already existing long position in the underlying financial instrument is called non-simultaneous covered writing or overwriting.

OPTION   A call option or a put option can be simply called an option.

OUT-OF-THE-MONEY   An option is said to be out-of-the money if exercising it and immediately closing the resulting position in the underlying financial instrument in the market would result in a loss.

PROFIT/LOSS PROFILE   The relationship between the profits or losses on a given position and the price of the underlying financial instrument is called the Profit/Loss Profile of that position.

PROTECTIVE PUT   A put option purchased against (or in other words, in addition to) a long position in the underlying financial instrument is called a protective put.

PUT OPTION   A contract that gives an investor the right to sell a financial instrument at a fixed price during a fixed period of time to another investor is called a put option or simply a put.

RECONVERSION   A position consisting of a short underlying financial instrument and an equal number of long calls and short puts on that financial instrument with the same strike price and the same expiration date is called a reconversion, a reverse conversion or a short conversion.

REWARD/RISK RATIO   The ratio of the gain an investor makes in his position when his forecast proves to be right to the maximum loss he incurs when his forecast proves to be wrong is called the Reward/Risk Ratio of that position.

SELLING OPTION   A transaction in which an investor sells the option which he owns is called selling the option. Selling options must not be confused with writing options.

SELLING SHORT   A transaction in which an investor sells a financial instrument or a commodity that he does not own is called selling short. In order to execute a short sale, the investor's broker borrows the financial instrument or the commodity and sells it in the investor's account. The investor undertakes the obligation to cover the position by buying the financial instrument or the commodity in the market upon the broker's request.

SHORT CALL   The position resulting from writing a call option is called a short call.

SHORT COMBINATION   The position resulting from writing an equal number of calls and puts on the same financial instrument with the same expiration date but with different strike prices is called a short combination.

SHORT PUT   The position resulting from writing a put option is called a short put.

SHORT STOCK   The position resulting from selling a stock short is called a short stock.

SHORT STRADDLE   The position resulting from writing an equal number of calls and puts on the same financial instrument with the same expiration date and the same strike price is called a short straddle.

SIMULTANEOUS COVERED WRITING   The strategy consisting of buying a financial instrument and immediately writing calls on this instrument is called simultaneous covered writing or buy-writing.

SPREAD   A position that consists of different long and short calls or different long and short puts on the same financial instrument is called a spread.

STOP-LOSS   An order placed with the broker that requires automatic closing of a position in a financial instrument when that instrument reaches a particular price is called a stop-loss or a stop-loss order. The price that triggers closing of the position under a stop-loss order is also called a stop-loss.

STRADDLE   A position consisting of an equal number of calls and puts on the same financial instrument with the same expiration date and the same strike price is called a straddle.

STRIKE PRICE   See exercise price.

TIME VALUE   The excess of the market price of an option over its intrinsic value is called its time value.

UNCOVERED OPTION   A short position in an option is called uncovered if exercising of that option would lead to the position in the underlying financial instrument which cannot be immediately covered through either the delivery of the instrument or through exercising another option.

UNDERLYING INSTRUMENT   The instrument that is bought or sold when an option contract is being exercised is called the under-lying instrument.

VERTICAL SPREAD   A position consisting of a number of long and short calls or long and short puts on the same underlying financial instrument with the same expiration date but different strike prices is called a vertical spread.

WRITING CALLS   Undertaking the obligation to sell a financial instrument on demand at a fixed price during a fixed period of time is called writing a call option (or simply a call) on that instrument.

WRITING COMBINATIONS   Writing an equal number of calls and puts on the same financial instrument with the same expiration date but different strike prices is called writing a combination.

WRITING PUTS   Undertaking the obligation to buy a financial instrument on demand at a fixed price during a fixed period of time is called writing a put option (or simply a put) on that instrument.

WRITING STRADDLES   Writing an equal number of calls and puts on the same financial instrument with the same expiration date and the same strike price is called writing a straddle.

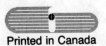

Printed in Canada